OXFORD BIBLE SERIES

General Editors
P. R. Ackroyd and G. N. Stanton

OXFORD BIBLE SERIES

General Editors
P. R. Ackroyd and G. N. Stanton

Prophecy and the Biblical Prophets

JOHN F. A. SAWYER

OXFORD UNIVERSITY PRESS
1993

Oxford University Press, Walton Street, Oxford OX2 6DP
Oxford New York Toronto
Delhi Bombay Calcutta Madras Karachi
Kuala Lumpur Singapore Hong Kong Tokyo
Nairobi Dar es Salaam Cape Town
Melbourne Auckland Madrid
and associated companies in
Berlin Ibadan

Oxford is a trade mark of Oxford University Press

Published in the United States
by Oxford University Press Inc., New York

British Library Cataloguing in Publication Data
Data available

Library of Congress Cataloging in Publication Data
Prophecy and the biblical prophets/John F. A. Sawyer.—Rev. ed.
(Oxford Bible series)
Includes bibliographical references and indexes.
1. Prophets. 2. Bible. O.T.—Prophets—Criticism,
interpretation, etc. I. Sawyer, John F. A. Prophecy and the
prophets of the Old Testament. II. Title. III. Series.
BS1505.2.S27 1993 224'.06—dc20 92-44095
ISBN 0-19-826210-8
ISBN 0-19-826209-4

1 3 5 7 9 10 8 6 4 2

Typeset by Best-set Typesetter Ltd., Hong Kong
Printed in Great Britain
on acid-free paper by
Biddles Ltd. Guildford and King's Lynn

FOR DEBORAH

GENERAL EDITORS' PREFACE

There are many commentaries on individual books of the Bible, but the reader who wishes to take a broader view has less choice. This series is intended to meet this need. Its structure is thematic, with each volume embracing a number of biblical books. It is designed for use with any of the familiar translations of the Bible; quotations are normally from RSV, but the authors of the individual volumes also use other translations or make their own where this helps to bring out the particular meaning of a passage.

To provide general orientation, there are two volumes of a more introductory character: one will consider the Old Testament in its cultural and historical context, the other the New Testament, discussing the origins of Christianity. Four volumes deal with different kinds of material in the Old Testament: narrative, prophecy, poetry/psalmody, wisdom and law. Three volumes handle different aspects of the New Testament: the Gospels, Paul and Pauline Christianity, the varieties of New Testament thought. One volume looks at the nature of biblical interpretation, covering both Testaments.

The authors of the individual volumes write for a general readership. Technical terms and Hebrew or Greek words are explained; the latter are used only when essential to the understanding of the text. The general introductory volumes are designed to stand on their own, providing a framework, but also to serve to raise some of the questions which the remaining volumes examine in closer detail. All the volumes other than the two general ones include discussion of selected biblical passages in greater depth, thus providing examples of the ways in which the interpretation of the text makes possible deeper understanding of the wider issues, both historical and theological, with which the Bible is concerned. Select bibliographies in each volume point the way to further discussion of the many issues which remain open to fuller exploration.

P.R.A.
G.N.S.

ACKNOWLEDGEMENTS

The author wishes to acknowledge assistance from the Department of Middle Eastern Studies, University of Melbourne, and the Research Fund of the University of Newcastle upon Tyne.

NOTE

CONTENTS

KEY PASSAGES DISCUSSED

The Phenomenon of Prophecy

PROPHETS are first and foremost 'proclaimers'. This seems to be the primary meaning of the Hebrew word *nabi*, as applied to the vast majority of biblical prophets. In most cases they were believed to have supernatural powers, but they are distinguished from diviners, sorcerers, necromancers, and the like, for which various other Hebrew terms are regularly used (cf. Deut. 18: 10–11). Their special status is indicated by two other distinctive terms used in a number of passages, 'men of God' (e.g. 1 Sam. 9; 1 Kgs. 13) and 'servants of God' (e.g. 2 Kgs. 21: 10; 24: 2). But the chief word throughout the Hebrew Bible is *nabi*, and it is a measure of the distinctiveness of the phenomenon that the word has been borrowed by English, where 'nabi' and 'nabism' are occasionally used in preference to the nearest English equivalents. It is significant too that the earliest Greek translators chose to translate *nabi*, not by the word *mantis* (from which words like 'necromancy' are derived), but by *prophetes* 'interpreter', from which our English word 'prophet' is derived (e.g. 1 Cor. 12: 29). 'Prophecy' means both prediction (foretelling) and proclamation (forthtelling), so that 'prophets' include not only people with supernatural powers, able like Cassandra, for example, to foresee events in the future, but preachers like St Francis of Assisi, John Wesley, Martin Luther King and other 'proclaimers' as well.

'The Prophets' is also the title of part of the Bible. In most English versions, which are based on the ancient Jewish translation of the Hebrew Bible into Greek, there are five books of the Prophets, corresponding to the five books of Moses: four Major Prophets (Isaiah, Jeremiah, Ezekiel, and Daniel) and the book of the twelve Minor Prophets (Hosea to Malachi). This 'prophetic Pentateuch' in Christian tradition manifestly points forward toward future fulfilment. From the ox and the ass in the first verses of Isaiah to the coming of the prophet Elijah 'before the great and terrible day of the Lord' (Mal. 4: 5), prediction is an integral part of the biblical tradition of the 'prophets' as it has come down to us.

In the Hebrew Bible, which constitutes Jewish Scripture, 'the Prophets' come between the 'Law' and the 'Writings' and refer to something different. The 'Former Prophets' include Joshua, Judges, Samuel and Kings as well, partly because the authors of these books were evidently not historians but religious writers, and partly because prophets like Deborah, Samuel, Elijah, Jonah, Isaiah, and many other 'men and women of God', named and unnamed, play so prominent a part in the narrative. The 'Latter Prophets' comprise only Isaiah, Jeremiah, Ezekiel, and the twelve, since Daniel is not reckoned as one of the Major Prophets and is grouped with the 'Writings' in the third part of the Bible.

The significance of the phenomenon of prophecy and the influence of these 'prophets' upon the religion of Israel and thus, ultimately, through Judaism, Christianity, and Islam, upon the whole world, cannot be overestimated. Julius Wellhausen, in one of his best known epigrams, stated that 'the Law [i.e. the Pentateuch] is later than the Prophets', arguing that the prophets came at the beginning of the history of the Israelite religion, not the end. However that may be, and however fitting the present arrangement of our Bibles may be, with the Prophets leading into the Gospels, it is more than likely historically that it was the ethical faith of the prophets that gave Israel's religion its distinctive stamp. The immense significance of the phenomenon of Israelite prophecy, one of the most dynamic and creative movements in the history of religion, makes it imperative that our study should begin with the phenomenon itself, within the history of Israel in particular.

This will lead us into a world of lonely mystics and miracle-workers, often 'despised and rejected by men' (Isa. 53: 3), and a world of clashes between the divine authority claimed by these charismatic figures, and the human authority of kings and human institutions. We shall be confronted by the highly sophisticated, often enigmatic, language of the prophets. The literary sources, both in the Bible and in what extrabiblical sources from the ancient world are available, present problems too. The texts were never intended as source material for reconstructing a picture of ancient Israelite society. The words of the prophets were recorded for teaching purposes, or for liturgical purposes, but seldom if ever as historical records as we would understand them. Their autobiographies, where we have them, evidently stress the divine authority they claimed to possess. Their extraordinary achievements, such as miracle-working, foretelling the future, intervening in political affairs, are much coloured by the hindsight of later generations. We will make allowance for such distorting factors, and make use of parallels, both ancient and modern, to the kind of mystical experiences referred to in the Bible, the supernatural powers they are depicted as possessing, and the peculiar role they seem to have played in ancient Israel.

Prophets appear in all parts of the Bible, from Balaam before Israel settled in Canaan (Num. 22–24) to Haggai, Zechariah and Malachi after the Babylonian Exile (586–538 BC). Nor must we forget, in the present context, that, despite the widespread belief that after these three 'the age of prophecy' ended, there continued to be men and women in ancient Judaism as elsewhere who claimed to be, and who were acknowledged to be, prophets. According to traditional Jewish belief, going back to Ecclesiasticus (*c.*180 BC), who stops at 'the Twelve' and omits Daniel (49: 10), with the departure of Malachi the 'spirit of prophecy' ceased to be active in Israel because no human beings were worthy to receive it. Instead God revealed his will by means of the *bat qol*, a disembodied 'heavenly voice' not communicated to or by any special individual who would then become a 'prophet'.

The modern distinction between prophecy and apocalyptic has also tended to perpetuate this view that 'the age of prophecy' ended with Malachi, in spite of the fact that Joel, Daniel and probably Isaiah 24–27 come from a later period than Malachi. In fact the distinction is not always a helpful one (see pp. 89 f.). The story of biblical prophecy must go on beyond Malachi into the Gospels where people hail both John the Baptist (e.g. Luke 1: 76; 7: 24 f.) and Jesus (e.g. Luke 7: 16; John 7: 40) as prophets, and into the early church where 'prophecy' is considered one of the 'gifts of the spirit' (e.g. 1 Cor. 12: 10), and the Book of Revelation is described as 'prophecy' (Rev. 1: 3; 22: 7). Another indication that the age of prophecy did not end with Malachi, is the presence among early Christian writings of the 'Sibylline Oracles', which purport to contain the utterances of Greek women prophets known as Sibyls (see p. 19).

A history of biblical prophecy must take account of all this, on the one hand noting developments and changing roles over the period, and, on the other, meticulously scrutinizing the text with a view to distinguishing between those elements most likely to be based on historical fact and those reflecting the ideas and beliefs of later generations. Thus, for example, the writer who represents Abraham as a prophet (Gen. 20: 7) is drawing on his familiarity with prophets or tales of prophets current in his own day. Nevertheless it is possible to identify in the Bible the main characteristics of this remarkable phenomenon, common to its earliest manifestations and to the last examples before its final decline, and, at the risk of over-simplification, we shall begin with a comprehensive analysis of the phenomenon of prophecy in ancient Israel.

The prophetic experience

The prophets' biographies or autobiographies, where we have them, normally contain some reference to their first mystical experience of God. In using the word 'mystical' one can usefully group together several varieties of experience, both 'prophetic', like the visions of Isaiah, and 'apocalyptic', like those of Daniel (see pp. 115–18), which have much in common. Let us take as our first example Isaiah's celebrated vision 'in the year that King Uzziah died' (6: 1–7). In this he is for an unforgettable moment permitted to see and hear what is going on in the heavenly court where God and his divine courtiers are engaged in dialogue. The scene recurs in various forms elsewhere in biblical tradition— 1 Kgs. 22: 19–23 is the most elaborate example (see pp. 11–13)— and is alluded to in Jer. 23: 18–22, Amos 3: 7, and elsewhere. It has much in common with the descriptions of the vision that Moses and the elders had of God in Exod. 24: 9–11, and the prologue to the book of Job, where the author and the reader are granted a secret glimpse behind the scenes (Job 1: 6–12; 2: 1–6). It also has much in common with the more elaborate 'apocalyptic' descriptions from a later age of the experiences of individuals like Enoch, Daniel, Paul (2 Cor. 12: 1–4), and John of Patmos (Rev. 1: 1–3; 22: 18–19). The scene is substantially the same in each case: privileged individuals see into the 'open heaven' (cf. John 1: 51).

The form of the narrative is affected by the writer's purpose. He may wish to emphasize the fact of the experience rather than its verbal or visionary content. This is true, for example, of Jeremiah's claims that the false prophets had not 'stood in the council of the Lord' (23: 18), with the implication that he himself had. Apocalyptic literature developed the imagery and symbolism of the description. Medieval writers attempted to analyse the 'dark night of the soul', perhaps to help others to cope with the experience if it happened to them. Others wished to glorify an individual saint. In the case of Job 1–2, the description is almost incidental to the main story, while in Daniel it is a measure of the martyr's faith in times of crisis. In the case of the biblical prophets, mystical experiences of this kind are recorded with one primary aim, the authentication of their message. But behind this variety of literary form the reality of the prophet's experience can hardly be questioned.

Another recurring theme in the descriptions of the prophets' experience is the inner compulsion that forces them to prophesy even when they try not to. Balaam is a good example of this (see pp. 71–2), his path supernaturally barred by the angel of the Lord (Num. 22: 21–35), and his prophecy, try as he might, completely under God's control:

And Balak said to Balaam, 'What have you done to me? ... I called you to curse my enemies, and behold, you have blessed them these three times ...'. And Balaam said to Balak, 'Did I not tell your messengers whom you sent to me. If Balak should give me his house full of silver and gold, I would not be able to go beyond the word of the Lord, to do either good or bad of my own will; what the Lord speaks, that will I speak.' (Num. 23: 11; 24: 10–12)

Another example is Jonah, who could not escape from the compulsion to speak God's word to the citizens of Nineveh. In the words of Amos, 'The Lord God has spoken, who can but prophesy?' (3: 8). Jeremiah's experience is discussed on p. 102.

There are also passages in which the sheer terror or spiritual turmoil of the experience is described, sometimes in great detail:

> A stern vision is told to me . . .
> Therefore my loins are filled with anguish;
>   pangs have seized me,
>   like the pangs of a woman in travail;
> I am bowed down so that I cannot hear,
>   I am dismayed so that I cannot see.
> My mind reels, horror has appalled me;
>   the twilight I longed for
>   has been turned for me into trembling.
>   (Isa. 21: 1–4; cf. Jer. 4: 19; Ezek. 1: 28; 3:
>   12 ff.; Hab. 3: 16).

Eliphaz the Temanite describes his vision in equally eerie language:

> Now a word was brought to me stealthily,
>   my ear received the whisper of it.
> Amid thoughts from visions of the night,
>   when deep sleep falls on men,
> dread came upon me, and trembling,
>   which made all my bones shake.
> A spirit glided past my face;
>   the hair of my flesh stood up.
> It stood still,
>   but I could not discern its appearance.
> A form was before my eyes;
>   there was silence, then I heard a voice . . .
>   (Job 4: 12–16)

The last line contains the same words as 1 Kgs. 19: 12 (see below). Daniel (8: 27; 10: 15 ff.) adds further graphic details to these accounts of human reactions to divine relevation.

Finally, lest it should be argued that these descriptions are the products of later, more sophisticated literary erudition, and do not represent actual experience (on the part of the author or the individual he is writing about), let us look at two striking cases from what is widely held to be the earliest stratum of prophetic biography, Balaam and Elijah. The formula with which Balaam's two most celebrated oracles begin appears to give us a glimpse into the prophetic experience:

> The oracle of Balaam the son of Beor,
>> the oracle of the man whose eye is opened [or closed? or perfect?],
> the oracle of him who hears the words of God,
>> who sees the vision of the Almighty,
>> falling down, but having his eyes uncovered.
>>> (Num. 24: 3–4; 15–16)

The language is striking and in some respects obscure; but we can be reasonably confident that it is ancient, not only because of the obscurity of the language used, but also because it is integral to the words of the prophet himself (see pp. 71–2).

The well-known passage in 1 Kings 19 in which a confrontation between Elijah and the Lord is represented in terms of a great wind, an earthquake, a fire, and a 'sound of thin silence' must in view of the previous discussion be understood as another description of the spiritual tumoil and mysterious dread of a prophet. The widely held view that 'the still small voice' (RSV) was the voice of the Lord instructing Elijah to have recourse to quiet persuasion instead of the spectacular, is rendered extremely improbable by two considerations. In the first place, there is a distinction between the series of phenomena referred to in vv. 11–12 and the coming of the voice of the Lord in v. 13. This implies that the fourth phenomenon was a mysterious sound rather than a voice: 'a sound of thin silence' rather than the 'still small voice' of tradition (the same Hebrew word can be translated 'sound' and 'voice' depending on the context: cf. Gen. 3: 8). The voice came later, after the prophet had responded to the divine revelation by wrapping his face in a mantle and going out to stand at the entrance of the cave (v. 13).

The other argument against the usual view that the 'still small voice' in v. 12 symbolizes the content of the subsequent words revealed to Elijah, is that what the Lord actually said to Elijah was, in effect, 'Go, anoint Hazael, Jehu and Elisha to slay all the Israelite worshippers of Baal' (vv. 15–16)—hardly quiet persuasion! Support for this interpretation of 1 Kgs. 19: 12 comes from a medieval Jewish commentator. Rashi tells us that the usual view in his day (twelfth-century France) was that it meant 'the sound of private prayer', although he himself favours the view that it refers to the 'ringing in the ears' (tinnitus) that you, but no one else, can hear. These are both attempts to understand what the mysterious experience of communion with God really is. 'The sound of thin silence' may be a paradox: it is certainly a striking and enigmatic expression, but its closest parallel is the vision of Eliphaz already referred to (Job 4: 13–16), as well as other attempts to describe the indescribable.

Not every prophetic biography contains the full description of such an experience. But it is implied in every case where the formula 'the word of the Lord came to...' is used. The verb translated 'came' in this expression, *hayah* in Hebrew, implies that something happened, or 'came to pass'. 'Oracle of the Lord' (RSV 'Thus says the Lord') has the same effect. Another indication in many cases is the reference to the time when the event or the experience took place: e.g. 'at the end of ten days' (Jer. 42: 7); 'in the second year of Darius the king, in the sixth month, on the first day of the month' (Hag. 1: 1); 'in the year that King Uzziah died' (Isa. 6: 1).

Even more dramatic are expressions like the spirit of God 'is upon me' (Isa. 61: 1; cf. Luke 4: 18) or 'took possession of...' (e.g. Judg. 6: 34) or 'came mightily upon...' (Judg. 14: 6, 19; 1 Sam. 10: 6, 10) or 'fell upon...' (e.g. Ezek. 11: 5), and 'the hand of the Lord...came upon...' e.g. 'Now the hand of the Lord had been upon me the evening before the fugitive came; and he had opened my mouth by the time the man came to me in the morning...' (Ezek. 33: 22; cf. 37: 1; Isa. 8: 11; Jer. 15: 17).

Again it must be emphasized that these expressions, widely distributed throughout the prophetic literature, do not prove the historicity of every example; but they do provide all the evidence we need for the historicity of the phenomenon. There is further-more every indication that the experience, call it ecstasy, trance, or inspiration, mystical or prophetic, was common to all the prophets, and attempts to distinguish a more primitive state in which ecstasy was the rule, from a later 'classical' stage where the spirit was less in evidence and the ecstasy rare, are not borne out by the evidence. It is true that references to 'the spirit of God' are rare in Jeremiah, but the experience is there (e.g. 1: 4 ff.; 15: 17; 20: 9), and in other respects he is absolutely typical of the phenomenon.

Divine possession

A passage of enormous significance for our understanding of the outward manifestations of prophecy is Num. 11: 16–30. The incident of the seventy elders prophesying is recounted as a demonstration of God's power. Like other prophets, notably Elijah, Jeremiah, and Jonah, Moses fears that he cannot cope with his lonely role as mediator between God and his people (v. 14) and appeals to God for help. The miracle of the prophesying elders and the miracle of the quails in the second part of the chapter are presented as the answer he receives, and the effect the spectacle has on the onlookers tells us much about the phenomenon as it was observed in ancient Israel.

In the first place, it is described as an act of divine intervention (vv. 24–5). Divine possession is regularly described in relation to the judges as well as the prophets (cf. Judg. 3: 10; 11: 29; 14: 6, 19), but the mysterious nature of the elders' behaviour here is implied by several unusual expressions. The spirit is not merely the spirit of the Lord transmitted directly from the deity to human agents, as in the examples from Judges, but some of the spirit which was already on Moses is taken and placed upon the elders. The term translated 'taken' (vv. 17, 25) occurs only here and looks like an isolated relic of ancient semi-technical language. There is a rich selection of normal Hebrew expressions for divine posses-sion which might have been used here. The unique expression heightens the numinous effect of the description. The same effect is carried over into the second section of the chapter, which begins with the word *ruaḥ* YHWH 'the wind/spirit of the Lord' (v. 31). 'Prophesying' (verbal form of the noun *nabi*) in this passage and elsewhere (e.g. 1 Sam. 10; Joel 2: 28) is a mysterious form of divine possession: NEB translates 'they fell into a prophetic ecstasy' (v. 25).

Another interesting feature of this description of prophesying is that it was contagious at a distance. Two men who had not been selected initially and had remained behind in the camp when the 'prophesying' took place were caught up in the same experience. The same thing happens to Saul in 1 Samuel 10 and 19; and we can assume that this was a not infrequent effect of the phenomenon. Such ecstasy or trance-like behaviour can spread through a community like a disease as the playwright Arthur Miller so convincingly illustrates in *The Crucible* (1952), a play based on the Salem witchcraft trials of 1692.

The effect on the rest of the community must have been even more marked. It aroused opposition or fear: Joshua at first called upon Moses to restrain the prophesying elders: 'My lord Moses, stop them!' He is of course rebuked by Moses, and his opposition is even more savagely crushed in another incident in the next chapter. These two incidents faithfully reflect the opposition, often violent, that must have existed both between rival groups of prophets (cf. 1 Kgs. 9: 22; Jer. 23) and between prophets and the rest of the community. Outward manifestations of divine possession were not always a guarantee that the prophets were respected: many were feared, their gifts resented, their authority rejected (cf. p. 19).

Finally, 'they prophesied. But they did so no more' (v. 25). This was a once and for all manifestation, but its effect was to equip the seventy with divine authority, equal to that of Moses, not just on that one occasion, but for ever. The authority invested in the seventy by that prophetic experience became a permanent feature of Israelite society and the biblical basis for the supreme council at Jerusalem, the Sanhedrin. Exactly what were the actual manifestations described as 'acting like a *nabi*'—speaking in tongues or the like—the text does not say. But it was recognized by the community as evidence of divine possession, and every *nabi* from that time on had his supporters and opponents, like any other religious authority.

Prophetic symbolism and second sight

We come now to what are variously referred to as 'symbolic acts', 'acted signs' (cf. Isa. 20: 3) or 'prophetic drama'. 1 Kings 22 contains one of the best known biblical examples. Four hundred or so court prophets are summoned before the kings of Israel and Judah to give advice on military strategy. The scene is Samaria, the kings, seated on their thrones, arrayed in their robes, at the entrance to the city, and the prophets 'prophesying before them' (i.e. behaving ecstatically: cf. Num. 11). Among them was one Zedekiah son of Chenaanah, who had made for himself iron horns, symbols of strength and aggression (Ps. 18: 2; Deut. 3: 17): 'With these you will gore the Syrians till you make an end of them' (v. 11). All the other prophets, each perhaps with his own parabolic visual aid, prophesied the same. Again this type of behaviour is not restricted to the early prophets in Samuel and Kings: Isaiah 20, Jeremiah 13 and 18, and Ezekiel 12 all contain striking examples as well.

There are two aspects to this phenomenon. In the first place it underlines the unique impact of such figures upon their contemporaries. Whatever their message, true or false (in 1 Kings 22 it happens to be false), they were extraordinary men whose behaviour drew attention to them and assured them of a permanent place in their society's records. It is also important to realize, however, that there is evidence from other societies, ancient and modern, that such parabolic behaviour not only made the point come home dramatically to onlookers, but was actually believed to affect the course of events. By acting this way, Zedekiah and his associates believed they were ensuring Israel's victory over the Syrians, because the word of God, whether spoken or acted by his prophets, is true and will be fulfilled. The term 'sympathetic magic' is sometimes used to describe this phenomenon. One thinks also of the effect that the practice of sticking pins in

somebody's effigy is believed to have on that person. There is no
need to doubt that, among the diviners and soothsayers of ancient
Israel as in other societies, such a belief was to be found.

But in the biblical narratives the phenomenon is far removed
from the realm of magic and wizardry, so emphatically banned in
Mosaic legislation (Deut. 18). It is presented as no more than a
dramatic alternative to the spoken word. The power in these signs
came from the Lord not from the actions themselves. It is therefore not surprising that such 'acted parables', with none of the
occult associations of their pagan precursors, are quite common in
the Writing Prophets. Isaiah went about naked and barefoot to
symbolize the humiliating defeat of Egypt and Ethiopia (20),
Jeremiah smashed a potter's vessel to represent the destruction
about to befall Jerusalem (19), and Ezekiel broke through the wall
of his house, took up his baggage and carried it out by night, to
represent the defeat and exile of his city (12). More elaborate
examples include the names Isaiah and Hosea gave to their children (Isa. 7–8; Hos. 1), and the action of Jeremiah in buying a
field at Anathoth (32). Hosea's marriage to Gomer (Hos. 1–3) is
probably another example. In each case it is clear that the action is
initiated by Yahweh in exactly the same way as the spoken word
'came to the prophet', and the emphasis is upon God's control
over events, rather than upon sympathetic magic in the prophets'
actions.

The second part of 1 Kings 22 tells of another prophet, Micaiah
ben Imlah, and the ways in which he received the word of God.
First he ridicules the false prophets, Zedekiah and the rest,
who prophesy to please the kings. Like Balaam and Jeremiah, he
speaks the word of the Lord, whether it pleases the king or not.
His answer is in two parts. The first illustrates a second technique
by which the prophet, with 'second sight', sees, in an everyday
object or scene, some hidden reality relevant to the occasion. Here
Micaiah sees a flock of sheep scattered on a hillside without a
shepherd, and this picture of leaderless vulnerability tells him that
Israel will certainly be defeated if they go to war with Syria. They
too have no leader, a direct and pointed insult to the kings in his
audience.

This technique for telling the future is documented in other societies, notably in travellers' tales from Arabia. In his invaluable book *Prophecy and Divination*, Alfred Guillaume tells how a wandering soothsayer came into a bedouin family encampment and was able to predict with impressive accuracy that a member of the family was about to give birth to a child, and even to predict its sex. The interesting part of the acccount is the soothsayer's explanation of how he did it. When he was asked for a prediction, he said his eye fell upon a water pot, *haml* in Arabic, which also means a pregnant woman; and when asked about the child's sex, his eye lit upon a cock sparrow which told him it was going to be a boy. This exact technique is recorded in Amos 7–8 and Jeremiah 1, a further indication of the accuracy and consistency of the biblical accounts of prophecy.

Micaiah's second answer is even more explicit. This time he recounts a visionary experience of a kind we have discussed above (p. 5). His glimpse into the workings of the heavenly court ('I saw the Lord sitting on his throne') not only authenticates his prophetic word to Israel, but also reveals to him (and to us) the complexity and diversity of the prophetic process. The Lord controls all the spirits that possess men, good and evil. False prophets, like Zedekiah, are possessed by lying spirits, sent by God to trick people, leading them, as in the case of Ahab, to their death. This interesting narrative is certainly the product of later speculation on the phenomenon of prophecy, in line with the Deuteronomic theology and legislation on pagan divination and wizardry. Extraordinary individuals, characterized by a variety of manifestations, were, or had been, familiar in Israelite society, and had to be accommodated to Yahwism.

Miracle-working

As well as the outward signs of divine possession, collectively described as 'prophesying' (cf. Num. 11: 25; see p. 9 above) and the ability to predict the future, miracle-working is an integral part of the phenomenon. Again it is the effect of the prophets' activities upon those about them that we can observe in the biblical records, not what they actually did. We are concerned with how the texts portray the prophets rather than with questions of historicity, and it is of very great importance to remember that miracle-working is part of the essence of the phenomenon, even though it figures less prominently in the 'Writing Prophets' than in the legends of Elijah and the rest of the historical narratives in Joshua–Kings. The emphasis in Isaiah, Jeremiah, Ezekiel, and the Twelve is on the words of the prophets rather than their actions, but their eccentric behaviour, their 'visions', and their ability to predict the future constitute a basic element in the way they are presented.

Almost as if to establish this point beyond any doubt, there is the enigmatic story of how Isaiah made 'the shadow cast by the declining sun on the dial of Ahaz turn back ten steps' (Isa. 38: 8; cf. 2 Kgs. 20: 8–11). Whatever happened, if anything, the narrative presents Isaiah as a miracle-worker like Moses and Elijah. Moses is once more the biblical prototype. When he doubted whether the people would believe that God had appeared to him and listen to his words, he was told that he was going to be able to perform miracles, turning his staff into a snake and covering his hand with leprosy 'that they may believe' (Exod. 4: 1–9). In the event, Pharaoh is not convinced by these demonstrations of divine power (7: 13), nor yet by the even more impressive series of miracles known as the 'Plagues of Egypt' (7–12), but their purpose is always the same, to prove the miraculous powers of the prophet and the superior power of his God.

1 Kings 17 attributes four miracles to the prophet Elijah. First he predicts a severe drought in Samaria, a prediction which provides the tense background to the celebrated rain-making contest on Mount Carmel (chapter 18). The wording of the passage places the emphasis on the miraculous 'word' of the prophet: 'there will be neither rain nor dew these years except by my word' (v. 1). The elements are under the authority of the prophet. Whether or not he was a skilled meteorologist requiring no supernatural power is beside the point, as in the case of Joseph, who deliberately disclaims any human skill or wisdom (Gen. 41: 16). The accuracy of his prediction is such that he is credited with supernatural powers by the author and, in all probability, although we cannot prove this, by his contemporaries too.

Secondly there is the miracle of the ravens. Just as God sent a miraculous fish to rescue another prophet from danger (Jonah 2), so here he sends ravens to provide Elijah with bread and meat in the morning and the evening. Again the emphasis is on the word and its fulfilment, but the miracle itself has a different purpose. In this case it is witnessed by no one but the lonely prophet himself. It is thus the readers of the legend, not the prophet's audience or contemporaries, that are the ones to be impressed by the miracle. Later traditions add apocryphal miracle-working stories to the legends of the prophets, such as the flight of Habakkuk to Babylon with food for Daniel (Bel and the Dragon, 33 ff.) and the miracle of the clay birds brought to life by Jesus in the Gospel of Thomas and the Qur'ān (3: 42). But the process began at the very beginning and is an integral part of the biblical text.

In the third miracle, that of the widow's empty jar of meal and cruse of oil, the word of God is again central, but the effect on the widow is postponed by the tragedy of her son's death. Far from acknowledging God's power with amazement and gratitude, she turns angrily of Elijah and accuses him of killing her son, presumably by his awesome presence in her house: 'Have you come here that my sins should be remembered?' (v. 18). At this Elijah performs a fourth, even more spectacular miracle, the climax of this narrative, by bringing her son back from the dead. The text again focuses on the word of God, and interprets the miracle as proof that 'the word of the Lord spoken by the man of God is true' (v. 24). Compassion for the widow (v.20) is secondary, as are the moral issues raised in v. 18 and the question of what actually happened. The parallel account in the Elisha narrative (2 Kgs. 4) adds some details (e.g. 'mouth to mouth, eyes to eyes, hands on his hands . . . and the child's flesh grew warm' v. 34), but again the conclusion makes the same point: 'she came and fell at his feet bowing to the ground' (v. 37). In similar circumstances the people hail Jesus as 'a great prophet' after a healing-miracle in the city of Nain (Luke 7: 11–17).

These and other examples of miracle-working constitute one of the main ways by which society recognizes the prophet and acknowledges his power, in particular the truth and divine authority of his word. It may well be that ecstatic behaviour and miracle-working were at one time the chief things for which the prophets were remembered, and the words of secondary importance. Other wonders associated with the prophets include conjuring up two she-bears (2 Kgs. 2: 23 ff.), healing a leper (2 Kgs. 5), and making an axehead float (2 Kgs. 6: 1–7), things which have little or no moral or religious content. They merely add to the image of the prophets as possessing unusual powers. They stand at one end of the spectrum, with Isaiah, Jeremiah, and the 'Writing Prophets' at the other, but the important conclusion of the present argument is that the distinction is one of degree, not of kind. The word of God and its miraculous fulfilment are integral parts of the prophetic legends in Samuel and Kings, while the traditional characteristics of the prophets, miracle-working, prediction of the future, visions, and eccentric behaviour appear as integral parts of the prophetic traditions recorded in the Prophets Isaiah to Malachi. We are dealing with a single phenomenon throughout.

Predicting the future

The one piece of legislation on prophecy occurs in Deut. 18: 9–22. In it the prohibition of various pagan practices such as divination, necromancy, and other forms of sorcery has close parallels in other law codes (cf. Exod. 22: 18; Lev. 19: 26, 31), as well as in the cautionary tales of the misdeeds of Israel's leaders (e.g. 2 Kgs. 17: 17; 23: 24; 1 Sam. 28: 3–25). The supernatural gifts of the true prophets of the Lord, in particular their ability to predict the future, are actually indistinguishable from those of the prohibited soothsayers and sorcerers. Yet the nine terms used in vv. 10–11 are exclusively applied to pagan practices, and this indicates a clear distinction, in the eyes of the Israelite community at any rate, between legitimate and illegitimate practices.

In contrast to the sorcerers, 'God will raise up a prophet (*nabi*) like Moses from among yourselves'. *Nabi* is the first word in both verses 15 and 18. It is typical of Deuteronomic tradition to hold up the prophetic achievements of Moses as the chief yardstick against which to evaluate Israel's leaders (cf. 2 Kgs. 18: 6, 12; 23: 25). Here he is presented as the supreme prototype for Israelite prophecy. Details of his gifts and achievements, his authority, his

dialogue with God 'face to face', and the 'signs and wonders that
the Lord sent him to do in the land of Egypt' are given in his
obituary (34: 9–12). Elsewhere Moses fulfils the role of prophet,
without being labelled *nabi*: his call (Exod. 3), his miracle-working
(Exod. 7 ff.), his visions of the Almighty (Exod. 33: 18 ff.), his
intercession for his people (Exod. 32: 30 ff.). But in Deuteronomy
he is presented as primarily a *nabi*.

It is also in this context that the forward-looking dimension of
Mosaic prophecy is emphasized. In the first place, Deut. 18: 18
provides scriptural authority for an important branch of Messianism
to which we shall return later (see p. 69). But secondly, the
criterion for distinguishing true prophecy from false is stated to be
future fulfilment: 'if the word does not come to pass or come true,
that is a word which the Lord has not spoken; the prophet has
spoken presumptuously, you need not be afraid of him (v. 22) . . .
that same prophet shall die' (v. 20). This answer is clearly not a
practical one, designed to enable the community to identify a false
prophet at once and take the appropriate action, since it involves
waiting to see whether the prophecy in question comes true or not,
maybe a long time in the future. But it does make us aware of two
important issues, important that is to the author of Deuteronomy.
On the one hand, the fulfilment of prophecy is a major concern of
the Deuteronomist and he argues throughout that God is true to
his word. Writing probably in the mid-sixth century BC, he was
anxious to stress the fact that the destruction of Jerusalem in 586
BC was not a theologically intractable disaster but a fulfilment of
prophecy. God was true to his word as spoken by his servants the
prophets, and therefore Israel could depend on their God to
rescue them as he had always done in the past. This is surely the
point he is making here. This is not legislation except in form
and arrangement: it is instruction aimed at explaining what had
happened and encouraging the victims of disaster.

On the other hand, by singling out successful prediction of
the future as the only criterion for identifying true prophets in
preference to visions of the heavenly court (Jer. 23; Isa. 38: 7 ff.;
and p. 5), he pinpoints the one supernatural gift of the prophets
that makes their word relevant long after their death. The prophet
is first and foremost, according to this key passage, one who can

successfully predict the future. Moses, the model on which this passage and other Deuteronomic passages on prophecy are based, died before the main bulk of his teaching was fulfilled, his vision of a new world still bright (34: 7), and, in that respect, the whole Pentateuch, with such a Deuteronomic epilogue, has a forward-looking dimension. The author of the 'five books of Moses', in other words, was a prophet rather than a lawgiver.

But this aspect of prophecy is central to all the other prophetic traditions too. Throughout the whole history of Israel and Judah as recounted in Joshua to Kings, the theme of prophecy and fulfilment runs like a golden thread, giving it shape and direction. Josh. 6: 26 points forward to 1 Kgs. 16: 34; 1 Kgs. 13: 2–5 to 2 Kgs. 23: 16 ff.; and 1 Sam. 2: 22–36 to 1 Kgs. 2: 27. The eighth-century prophets are rooted in their historical context, partly to give their words this supernatural dimension. Thus, in chapters 40–55 Isaiah predicts the rebuilding of the already ruined city and the triumphant return of the exiles (see pp. 84–5 (or 6)). Amos does the same in chapter 9. The medium in which this prophecy and fulfilment is worked out is of course a literary process, and the historical question of whether eighth-century prophets actually predicted the Babylonian exile or whether Daniel in sixth-century Babylon predicted the Maccabean crisis with almost perfect accuracy, is not raised (see pp. 114–15). But the belief that such gifted, divinely possessed characters could accurately predict the future is a historical fact, an important element in the biblical pattern of prophetic behaviour, and one which for the Deuteronomist is clearly the most important.

The role of the prophet in society

The extraordinary experiences and manifestations that we have been considering had the effect of making the prophets instantly recognizable to their contemporaries. Not every prophet was characterized by exactly the same manifestations, but all had enough in common to be identifiable as prophets. Our next task is to examine the reaction of society to these people, the role they played, and their relationship to the institutions, the monarchy, the

Temple, the priesthood, and the education system of ancient Israel.

We might begin with the question, what would happen to such eccentrics in our own day? Some of them at any rate would undoubtedly be certified as insane. Others would be politely ignored. Others would be mercilessly laughed at. The only ones to survive long enough to make positive contributions to our society would be those protected by an institution (like the Church) or influential friends. It is important to remember that the situation in ancient societies was not so very different. The prophets in ancient Israel were locked up (e.g. Jer. 37), ignored (Isa. 6: 9 ff.), persecuted (2 Kgs. 17: 33), 'despised and rejected by men' (Isa. 53: 3). Without some protection or support they would not have survived either as individuals or as groups.

We can identify two types of institution in which individual prophets existed. The first is exemplified by the prophetess and judge Deborah, who 'used to sit under the palm of Deborah between Ramah and Bethel in the hill country of Ephraim; and the people of Israel came up to her for judgement' (Judg. 4: 5). Like the oracles at Delphi, Dodona, and elsewhere or the sibyls at Cumae and other sites, Deborah was a localized institution, officially consulted by the political and military authorities.

Balaam is another example of the same type of institution located at 'Pethor, which is near the River, in the land of Amaw' and consulted by the king of Moab (Num. 22: 5 ff.). Tradition associates a prophet with Bethel (1 Kgs. 13: 11 ff.), where one of the Bible's best-known and most spectacular visionary experiences took place (Gen. 28: 10–22), and where the Israelites consulted their oracle in the days of the judges (Judg. 10: 18; cf. also perhaps Amos 5: 5). Maybe there was a similar institution there. Samuel's association with Ramah (1 Sam. 7: 16–17; 19: 18–24; 28: 3) may be another example and the 'witch of Endor' another, consulted by Saul when 'the Lord did not answer him, either by dreams, or by Urim, or by prophets' (1 Sam. 28: 3–25). Even though the Bible contains few examples, such people, male and female, orthodox and heterodox, were probably quite familiar in ancient Israel, in spite of the attempts by Saul (1 Sam. 28: 3) and Josiah (2 Kgs. 23: 24) to abolish them. Equipped with various means of divination, surrounded by an aura of wonder and respect, and presumably paid a good price for their services, they survived.

The other institution in which such people were able to exist, for the most part untroubled by the hostility or scorn of society, was the royal court: Nathan at the court of David at Jerusalem, Elijah and Elisha at Samaria in the days of Ahab and Jezebel, Isaiah at Hezekiah's court, Huldah at Josiah's, and Jeremiah at that of the last kings of Judah before the fall of Jerusalem. Many of the individual prophets recorded in the literature of Israel's ancient neighbours are of this type. In the Mari texts (eighteenth century BC Syria) there are examples of the king consulting his own prophetic 'adviser', known as *apilum* 'answerer'. Wen Amon, an Egyptian traveller writing in about 1000 BC, describes the prophetic ecstasy of a member of the court of the prince of Byblos in Phoenicia, and the Neo-Assyrian kings regularly consult their court prophets at Nineveh. Such figures were often members of prophetic guilds or groups, and this brings us to another type of institution in which prophets existed in Israelite society.

There is good evidence, both in the Bible and in other ancient near eastern texts, for associations or guilds of prophets. We have already mentioned the four hundred prophets at the court of the king of Israel (1 Kgs. 22). Elijah's opponents in the celebrated contest on Mount Carmel were 'four hundred and fifty prophets of Baal and four hundred prophets of Asherah, who eat at Jezebel's table' (1 Kgs. 18: 19), clearly a recollection of how things were in the early monarchy.

Some interesting details of how these associations were organized can be gleaned from other legends. Members were known as 'sons of the prophets' (2 Kgs. 4: 38) and their leader possibly as 'father' (2 Kgs. 2: 12). Two possible technical terms for these guilds or associations occur in 1 Sam. 10: 5, 10 (*hebel* 'rope'?) and 1 Sam. 19: 20 (*lahaqa* 'company'). Leaders of such groups include Samuel (1 Sam. 19: 20) and Elisha (2 Kgs. 6: 22), who apparently was accompanied by a servant, Gehazi (5: 20 ff.). The continuing existence of this institution, particularly in the northern kingdom, down into the eighth century BC, is attested by the words of Amos at Bethel: 'I am not a prophet nor the son of a prophet [i.e. a member of a prophetic guild]' (Amos 7: 14). Jeremiah 23 contains references to 'the prophets of Jerusalem' and 'the prophets of Samaria' which could be taken as evidence for prophetic guilds even in the sixth century.

At all events it is clear that in ancient Israel, while individual prophets appear regularly from Balaam in the earliest period down to Haggai and Zechariah after the Babylonian Exile, references to guilds of prophets belong mainly to the early monarchy. Extra-biblical evidence for such guilds comes from ancient Mesopotamia, where guilds of 'ecstatics' (under the leadership of the king) are regularly referred to, and, in more modern times, from the Muslim world, where 'schools' or 'fraternities' of dervishes are recorded.

We come now to the much discussed question of the relationship between prophet and cult. On the one hand, there are a good many passages in the prophetic literature which are violently critical of aspects of Israelite worship, e.g.:

> What to me is the multitude of your sacrifices?
>   says the Lord . . .
> I do not delight in the blood of bulls,
>   or of lambs, or of he-goats. . . .
> Bring no more vain offerings;
>   incense is an abomination to me. . . .
> Your new moons and your appointed feasts
>   my soul hates . . .
>
>   (Isa. 1: 11 ff.; cf. 66: 1–4)

Two passages go so far as to suggest, albeit rhetorically, that the sacrificial system is not part of original pure Mosaic religion (Jer. 7: 21 ff.; Amos 5: 25). Some prophets, notably Amos (7: 14), deliberately dissociate themselves from the cultic establishment. Confronted with a straight choice between 'burnt offerings' and 'obeying the voice of the Lord' (1 Sam. 15: 22) or between offering fatted beasts and aiming to 'let justice roll down like waters, and righteousness like an everflowing stream' (Amos 5: 24), the prophets, from Samuel on, choose obedience and justice.

Some modern Christian commentators, suspicious of ritualism in their own experience, have tended to over-emphasize the dichotomy between the prophets and the cult, between the free voice of prophecy and the dead hand of the institutions. But clearly there was no such sharp distinction. The evidence is overwhelming for a close connection between the prophet and the political and religious institutions, however critical the one may have been of the other.

In the first place, it is not only for the early period that our texts provide evidence for a close association between prophets and cult. Along with descriptions of the 'band of prophets coming down from the high place with harp, tambourine, flute and lyre before them, prophesying' in the days of Saul (1 Sam. 10: 5), and the consistent location of early prophets within the sanctuaries of Bethel, Ramah, and elsewhere referred to above, we must remember that it was at Bethel that Amos prophesied (7: 10–17), and in the Temple at Jerusalem that Jeremiah and Hananiah prophesied to 'the priests and all the people' (Jer. 28)—all bitter critics of the cult as we have seen. Furthermore, our texts tell us that several of the prophets were actually priests themselves. Jeremiah and Ezekiel are both introduced as members of priestly families, while Samuel was trained by Eli the priest at Shiloh. No doubt others came from a priestly background too, Haggai and Zechariah for example, whose preoccupation with cultic subjects and use of cultic language and imagery are remarkable.

There is no technical term for a cultic official whose function was to act as prophet in worship, although it does not seem impossible that the word *nabi* 'spokesman' had such a cultic meaning, to judge from the evidence we have just been considering and the juxtaposition of the term prophet and priest in several passages (e.g. Jer. 8: 10; 18: 18). The striking correspondence between the Hebrew term *kohen* 'priest' and its Arabic cognate *kahin* 'soothsayer/prophet' points to a common lexical ancestor meaning 'cultic prophet, prophet-priest', although *kohen* is not attested with this meaning in the Hebrew Bible. However that may be, there is one final type of evidence for the closest connection between prophet and cult in ancient Israel, namely the evidence of the texts.

On the one hand, the prophetic literature is full of liturgical material, like the psalms in Isaiah 38, Jonah 2, and Habakkuk 3, the hymns of praise and Enthronement Psalms in Deutero-Isaiah (see pp. 35–6), and the Individual Laments in Jeremiah 11–20. On the other hand, the book of Psalms contains even more remarkable evidence for a cultic official with a prophetic function. The evidence falls into two categories. First, there are passages in which the direct words of God are given, alongside those of the worshipping community: e.g. Psalm 60 introduces such words with the formula 'God has spoken in his sanctuary' (v. 6). Other 'oracles' in the book of Psalms include Ps. 50: 5, 81: 6 ff., 91: 14 ff., and 95: 8 ff. Was the priest with the duty of uttering the words of God in the original cultic setting of these psalms not in fact a 'prophet'?

The other type of evidence for such a functionary comes from a comparison of Deutero-Isaiah with the Psalms of Lamentation. Psalm 22 is a familiar example: the question we have to ask is what happened between v. 21 and v. 22? For twenty-one verses the psalmist cries to God for help, describing his plight in a series of unrelieved images of pain and terror. Then, from v. 22 on, he changes to a hymn of public praise and thanksgiving, almost as if his prayer has been answered somehow in the gap between v. 21 and v. 22. It has been convincingly argued that a 'salvation oracle' was originally delivered at this point in the ritual, and, what is even more interesting, that such oracles have been preserved, not in the book of Psalms, but in Deutero-Isaiah. Isaiah 43: 1 ff. is a beautiful example:

> Thus says the Lord . . .
> 'Fear not, for I have redeemed you;
>   I have called you by name, you are mine.
> When you pass through the waters, I will be with you;
>   and through the rivers, they shall not overwhelm you;
> when you walk through fire you shall not be burned,
> and the flame shall not consume you.'
>
> (cf. 41: 8 ff., 14; 44: 2 ff.)

Even more convincing would be the connection between the following:

> But I am a worm, and no man;
>   scorned by men, and despised by the people . . .   (Ps. 22: 6)

Fear not, you worm Jacob,
  you men of Israel!
I will help you, says the Lord;
  your Redeemer is the Holy One of Israel

                    (Isa. 41: 14)

It is certainly suggestive that, in addition to other cultic compositions in the prophetic literature, these salvation oracles originate in
a liturgical context too, and thus provide further evidence for the
link between prophet and cult.

One final issue involved in the debate on the relation between
prophet and cult is the education and training of the prophets. If it
could be shown, for example, that prophets were trained apart
from priests and other officials, then a considerable gap between
prophets and the cult might be opened up. But exactly the opposite
seems to have been the case. The overlaps that we have just been
considering between the prophetic and the liturgical literature,
together with the prophets' evident familiarity with life at court
and in the Temple, not to mention international politics and
current affairs, point in the direction of educated prophets, from a
background not dissimilar to that of other leaders, officials, and
members of the intelligentsia. However emphatically they may
protest their independence from the 'establishment', their style,
their knowledge, and their prominent role in society prove that
they belonged firmly to the religious, political, and educational
heart of ancient Israelite society.

What then was the distinction, if any, between the 'Writing
Prophets' and other prophets, both in Israel and in other societies?
The answer to which our discussion has been leading us is surely
that it was not in their behaviour, or in their role in society, or in
their education. They were just as much part of the establishment
as the rest of the prophets. It was the content of their teaching,
and one might add the content of their experience of God, that
marked them out as different. In the royal court, in the Temple,
among the priests and prophets and wise men of their day, the
prophets whose words and exploits are recorded with approval in
our texts stand out as unique, starting with Samuel among the
prophets at Ramah and culminating in the great, lonely figures of

Jeremiah and Ezekiel. Their opposition to the official cult came from their moral and religious convictions, not from their different social background or status.

There is one more factor that might have contributed to the survival of this remarkable phenomenon in ancient Israel. Did the prophets have circles of disciples to preserve their teachings and remember their exploits for prosperity? There is very little evidence. In the early legends, as we noted, there were groups of prophets clustered round a leader like Samuel and Elisha. But these are scarcely disciples, charged with preserving their master's words, and besides, such guilds are not documented for the period of the 'Writing Prophets'. Isa. 8: 16 is frequently quoted in this connection: 'Bind up the testimony, seal the teaching among my disciples'. This is actually the only reference to disciples in the whole corpus, and there are difficulties of interpretation. The verbs may not be imperative; the Hebrew for 'among my disciples' is anomalous and may mean 'with my teaching' (cf. NEB 'seal the oracle with my teaching'). It is certainly a very shaky foundation on which to build any theory that the prophets' words were preserved by their disciples. Jeremiah is the one exception: we are told that some of his words were recorded by Baruch (Jer. 36), but was he a disciple and not a scribe or even a government official?

The other relevant fact is the very existence of the prophetic books themselves. In particular, the book of Isaiah, which consists of sixty-six chapters, manifestly represents an accumulation of Isaianic tradition over a period of not less than 200 years. Even allowing for the exceptional impact of the original figure of Isaiah on eighth-century BC Jerusalem and the support he received at Hezekiah's court, someone must have taken it upon himself to preserve his teachings so that, in the reign of Josiah, during the Babylonian Exile, and probably at other times and in other places as well, they could be elaborately reinterpreted and extended. Perhaps 'the men of Hezekiah' who 'copied the proverbs of Solomon' (Prov. 25: 1) represent a well-established literary institution at Jerusalem, about which we unfortunately know practically nothing. We certainly know nothing about schools of disciples surrounding individual prophets, and the literary problems of transmission, collection, and redaction belong to another chapter.

2

The Prophetic Literature

THE literary form in which the prophets' words have come down to us has been the subject of much debate. At one time it was thought that the identification of distinctive types (*Gattungen*) of prophetic utterance might assist us in determining what such and such a prophet actually said. This historical optimism was soon found to be misplaced, however (as in the case of the sayings of Jesus), since an individual, to say what he wants to say, may or may not choose to employ a conventional type (priestly oracle, hymn, parable), and he may or may not change it with varying degrees of creativity and originality. Moreover, the authors of our texts or the disciples or the community responsible for transmitting the original words to us may do the same. Whatever the literary form, and however many parallels to it can be quoted from elsewhere in the Bible or the ancient world, there is no way that form criticism on its own can lead us to the actual words of the prophets.

Form criticism can, however, throw light on the origins and background of the prophets in ancient Israel, and in that respect has something to say about the historicity of the phenomenon. The fact that they did employ stereotyped literary forms proves that they had undergone some kind of training. As we shall see, they show considerable skill in handling sophisticated literary techniques, drawn from various sources, poetic, didactic, liturgical, or the like. This can give us some fascinating insights into the process whereby the original, uncanny, often disturbing experiences of a lonely prophet have been transformed into the rich and elaborate prophecies which make up the prophetic books as we now have them.

With these preliminary remarks on the limitations of form criticism, let us turn to the prophetic texts themselves, starting with the shortest and simplest utterances and moving from there to larger units, concluding with the final shape of the prophetic books themselves.

The oracle

The word 'oracle' is a technical term for various kinds of mysterious utterance delivered by a prophet in response to a worshipper's question. 'Consulting the oracle' refers to the ancient practice of visiting a sanctuary, such as the shrine of Apollo at Delphi, and engaging in appropriate rituals with a view to receiving divine guidance. It has been suggested that the visit of Jacob to a mysterious place, recognized by him as 'the gate of heaven', where he dreamt that the Lord promised to be with him always (Gen. 28: 10–22), is a biblical example. There are plenty of other less elaborate examples where the Lord is 'consulted' by his people in time of need (e.g. Judg. 1: 1 after the death of Joshua) and by individuals like Saul (e.g. 1 Sam. 14: 37) and David (e.g. 1 Sam. 23: 2; 30: 7–8).

Apart from isolated references to dreaming (e.g. 1 Sam. 25: 2; see also above on Gen. 28) and other means of divination involving the use of the ark of the covenant of God (Judg. 20: 27) and the enigmatic 'Urim and Thummim' (Deut. 33: 8, 1 Sam. 14: 41–2; 28: 6; Ezra 2: 63), little is known of ancient Israelite practice. But the role of prophets in the business of 'consulting the Lord' is clear enough, and the application of the word 'oracle' to their responses therefore appropriate. Deborah, sitting under her palm tree in the hill country of Ephraim, was one such prophet (Judg. 4: 4). Court prophets delivered oracles on demand, whether they were believed or not (e.g. 1 Kgs. 22). On more than one occasion during the siege of Jerusalem, Jeremiah was consulted by the king (21; 37: 3–10), as was Isaiah by King Hezekiah (Isa. 37: 5 ff.), and Ezekiel by the elders of Judah (e.g. Ezek. 14). Whatever else the prophets did, and however sophisticated the form of the prophetic literature as we now have it, they were first and foremost oracle-givers, that is to say transmitters of divine responses to human questions.

The Hebrew term translated 'oracle' in modern English versions (RSV, JB, NEB) is *massa* 'burden' (cf. Jer. 23: 33), and is applied to all manner of prophetic utterances from lengthy 'oracles concerning foreign nations' (e.g. Isa. 13: 1; 14: 28; 15: 1; 17: 1; 19: 1; 21: 1; 22: 1; 23: 1) and whole books (e.g. Nahum, Habakkuk, Malachi) to shorter prophecies addressed to specific situations (e.g. Ezek. 12: 10). It may be connected with the solemn lifting of the hand as when an oath is sworn, and, like the much more frequent terms translated 'the word of the Lord' and 'the very word of the Lord' (NEB for 'says the Lord' in Jer. 1: 8, 19; 2: 3; 3: 10; 13: 20, etc.), *massa* emphasizes the divine authority of the words and the prophetic experience behind them, but is too general for our purpose. We shall instead reserve the term 'oracle' for the basic unit around which the whole prophetic corpus is constructed.

It is likely that many such oracles originated in the prophet's experience in the form of a single striking word or phrase. We noted above the use of word-plays in the prophetic tradition (see p. 13). A word suggesting both 'summer' and 'end' sparked off the oracle in Amos 8: 1–2, and a word meaning both 'almond' and 'watchful' provided the inspiration for Jer. 1: 11–12. Prophecies are similarly built around the extraordinary names of Isaiah's sons, Shear Jashub (7: 3) and Mahershalalhashbaz (8: 1). The name Immanuel is probably another example (7: 10–17; cf. 8: 8, 10), as is the prophecy constructed out of the word 'house' in Amos 3: 13–15:

> 'Hear and testify against the *house* of Jacob,'
>   says the Lord God, the God of hosts,
> 'that on the day I punish Israel for his transgressions,
>   I will punish the altars of Bethel [Heb. '*house* of El'],
> and the horns of the altar shall be cut off
>   and fall to the ground.
> I will smite the winter *house* with the summer *house*;
>   and the *houses* of ivory shall perish,
> and the great *houses* shall come to an end,'
>   says the Lord.

Notice how the three meanings of the word 'house', family, temple, and private residence, are all related to the city of Bethel, where the prophecy was probably originally delivered.

From such prophetic 'embryos' let us move on now to the basic oracle itself. The commonest is the 'salvation oracle', which was God's comforting response to his people's cries for help. Its origin was in some kind of ritual at the temple, perhaps as the priests' answer to the prayers, confessions, and laments of the worshipper. As we saw above, it has been suggested that the abrupt change of mood in some of the Psalms, from despondency to jubilation (e.g. Psalm 22), is to be explained as due to the intervention of a priest or 'cultic prophet' (see pp. 23–4). But in spite of its liturgical origin, we have to look for examples in the prophetic literature rather than in Psalms. Why the oracles of the Lord are so rarely found in the Psalter is not hard to explain. The few examples, such as Pss. 2: 7–9, 60: 6–8, and 110: 1, 4 are exceptions, since the Psalms contain almost exclusively the hymns and prayers of the worshippers. The words of God in response to their cries are contained in the prophetic books. The psalmist prays:

> Arise, O Lord: O God lift up thy hand;
> forget not the afflicted.
> (Ps. 10: 12; cf. 3: 7; 94: 2)

The prophet replies, in a typical salvation oracle:

> Fear not, for I am with you,
> be not dismayed, for I am your God;
> I will strengthen you, I will help you,
> I will uphold you with my victorious right hand.
> (Isa. 41: 10; cf. 33: 10; 41: 14 ff.; 43: 1–7).

The formula 'fear not' is usually there, often at the beginning, and references to past acts of divine intervention on behalf of his people ('I am your God ... I have redeemed you ... I have called you in righteousness ...') lead into promises of future salvation ('I will be with you ... I will pour water on the thirsty land ...').

The oracle frequently ends with a statement about the nature and purpose of God's intervention, e.g. 'that men may see and know ... that the hand of the Lord has done this, the Holy One of Israel has created it' (41: 20). Examples can be quoted from the whole corpus of prophetic literature (e.g. Jer. 1: 6–8; 30: 10; 46: 3 ff.; Joel 2: 19–27). Jer. 15: 19–21 is a rare example in context, that is immediately after a lament (vv. 15–18). But nowhere is the salvation oracle more frequent than in the Babylonian chapters of the book of Isaiah (e.g. 33; 41; 43; 44; 49).

Messenger speech

Such oracles suggest a picture of the prophet in residence somewhere, and people coming to him to 'consult the oracle', in his house (e.g. Ezek. 14), or at some sacred site (e.g. Judg. 4: 4–5). The second literary type we shall examine presents the prophet as a messenger bringing the word of God to his people or his king. This is in fact the commonest form in which prophecy is recorded and clearly represents the chief way in which the prophet's role in ancient society was perceived. The earliest examples come from eighteenth-century BC Mari, a city on the upper Euphrates in eastern Syria. The opening formula is addressed to the prophet, e.g. 'Arise, go to Nineveh ...' (Jonah 1: 2); 'Go, tell Hananiah ...' (Jer. 28: 13). A beautiful elaboration of this is to be found in Isaiah 6: 'And I heard the voice of the Lord saying, "Whom shall I send, and who will go for us?" And I said, "Here am I! Send me". And he said, "Go and say to this people ..."' (see pp. 87–9).

In every case the prophet experiences the call to be God's messenger. The message itself is introduced by the words 'Hear this ...' or 'Listen ...' (e.g. Jer. 28: 15; Amos 3: 1). Again Isaiah 6 contains a striking variation: 'Hear and hear, but do not understand ...' (v. 9). Then comes a vivid description of how things are, or have been up to the present, e.g. 'because you have not obeyed my words' (Jer. 25: 8); 'because this people have refused the waters of Shiloah that flow gently' (Isa. 8: 6). This is followed by the main component of the prophecy, a prediction of what is going to happen, introduced by the words 'therefore ...' or

'But now . . .' (e.g. Jer. 42: 22; Hag. 2: 4; Zech. 8: 11). This is the point at which the familiar formula 'Thus says the Lord' frequently appears, as though to reinforce the awesome authority of the message brought by the prophet. These are not his words, but the very word of God. Finally there may be a concluding sentence of the same form as the ending to an oracle, e.g.:

> For lo, he who forms the mountains . . .
> the Lord, the God of hosts, is his name. (Amos 4: 13)

Amos 7 contains an impressive and familiar example of a prophetic messenger speech, delivered to the priest of Bethel:

(a)	Commission:	The Lord took me from following the flock and said to me, 'Go, prophesy to my people Israel'.
(b)	Summons:	Now therefore, hear the word of the Lord.
(c)	Past/present: situation	You say, 'Do not prophesy against Israel, and do not preach against the house of Isaac.'
(d)	Future prediction:	Therefore, thus says the Lord: 'Your wife shall be a harlot in the city and your sons and your daughters shall fall by the sword, and your land shall be parcelled out by line; you yourself shall die in an unclean land, and Israel shall surely go into exile away from its land'. (Amos 7: 15 ff.)

Many of the examples quoted are prophecies of judgement: the past or present situation is one of disobedience or corruption, and the prediction one of judgement. But there are also prophecies of salvation composed in this predominantly doom-laden form, which are all the more effective for that. Isaiah 37 contains an elaborate one:

Then Isaiah the son of Amoz sent to Hezekiah saying, 'Thus says the Lord, the God of Israel: Because you have prayed to me concerning

Sennacherib king of Assyria, this is the word that the Lord has spoken concerning him . . . He shall not come into this city, or shoot an arrow there, or come before it with a shield, or cast up a siege-mound against it . . . For I will defend this city to save it, for my own sake and for the sake of my servant David'. (vv. 21 ff.; 33 ff.)

A lengthy poem (vv. 22–9) and the mention of a sign (vv. 30 ff.) fill out the basic framework.

On the other hand the Immanuel prophecy in Isaiah 7 looks like a typical prophecy of judgement, addressed to a faithless and uncooperative king (7: 13–17), although later tradition transformed it, probably because of the name 'Immanuel' (= 'God is with us': 8: 10) into one of Messianic salvation (e.g. Matt. 1: 22–3), abandoning its original structure.

Other literary types

In addition to these two exclusively prophetic types of composition which account for a very large proportion of biblical prophecies, there is a considerable variety of what might be termed secondary types, that is to say types of literary composition derived from other sources and incorporated, by the prophet himself or an editor, into the prophetic literature as we now have it.

We begin with the so-called 'Woe-utterances'. There are six in Isaiah 5 and a seventh (probably at one time part of the same group) in chapter 10:

> Woe to those who decree iniquitous decrees,
>> and the writers who keep writing oppression,
> to turn aside the needy from justice
>> and to rob the poor of my people of their right,
> that widows may be their spoil,
>> and that they may make the fatherless their prey.
>
>> (vv. 1–2)

There are other examples in Jeremiah 22, Ezekiel 13, Micah 2, Nahum 3, Habakkuk 2, Zephaniah 3, and elsewhere. These seem originally to have been short, threatening speeches, almost like magical incantations, consisting of little more than lists of enemies or victims and their evil deeds. Often they are followed by prophecies of judgement, e.g.

> Woe to those who lie upon beds of ivory,
>   and stretch themselves upon their couches...
> Therefore they shall now be the first of those to go into exile.
>   (Amos 6: 4–7; cf. Isa. 5: 13 ff., 24 ff.)

Longer compositions like Isaiah 28, 29, 30, 31, and 33, which begin with the 'Woe...' formula, have only a very superficial connection with the original literary form. It has been suggested that these passages are the negative counterparts of the 'beatitudes', which have the same grammatical strucure: 'happy are those who...' (e.g. Ps. 1; 41; 119; 128; Prov. 3: 13 ff.; 8: 32 ff.; Job 5: 17; Matt. 5: 3 ff.), and that they both have a common origin in ancient didactic tradition. If this were so it would be hard to explain why 'Woe...' never appears in the wisdom literature, and 'Happy...' only three times in the prophets (Isa. 30: 18; 32: 20; 56: 2). A third theory regarding the origin of 'Woe...' passages is that they were originally funeral laments, bemoaning the fate of the victims as if they were already dead. But in view of what has been said above about the probable cultic and ecstatic roots of prophecy, the incantation theory is to be preferred.

There is no doubt about the original setting of the next type to be examined, the trial speeches. We should not make the mistake of assuming, however, that ancient lawcourts were conducted on similar lines to modern European ones. We should think instead of a crowded scene at the city gate, individuals putting their case in the crowd (Ruth 4), the king or his appointed officials available as an ultimate court of appeal in disputed cases (e.g. 2 Sam. 14; 1 Kgs. 3: 16–28; 2 Kgs. 6: 26). Experienced senior citizens like Job had a vital role to play (Job 29). The falsely accused could suffer at the hands of their enemies (e.g. Psalm 109; Isa. 29: 20 f.), and so could those without strong help 'at the gate' from family or friends (e.g. Job 5: 4; cf. Prov. 22: 22; Ps. 127: 5). The familiarity of this everyday scene made it a popular model for prophetic proclamation. Amos 3: 9 ff. is a short, graphic example:

(*a*) Proclaim to the strongholds of Ashdod,
    and to the strongholds in the land of Egypt,
and say, 'Assemble yourselves upon the mountains of Samaria,
and see the great tumults within her,
    and the oppressions in her midst.'

(*b*) 'They do not know how to do right,' says the Lord,
    'those who store up violence and robbery in their strongholds.'

(*c*) Therefore thus says the Lord God:
    'An adversary shall surround the land, and bring down your defences from you,
    and your strongholds shall be plundered.'

First, the crowds are summoned as witnesses (*a*), in this case Israel's western neighbours the Philistines and the Egyptians, pictured as taking their places on the hills overlooking Samaria. Then the case against the accused (Samaria) is stated (*b*) and finally the sentence passed (*c*). Often both (*b*) and (*c*) are spoken by God, and the sentence (*c*) is almost invariably prefaced by the formula, 'Therefore thus says the Lord. . . .'

A most effective development of this is the dispute in which God throws out a challenge to his adversary, e.g.:

Set forth your case, says the Lord;
    bring your proofs, says the King of Jacob . . . Tell us what
is to come hereafter,
    that we may know that you are gods . . . !'

(Isa. 41: 21 ff.)

Here the adversaries are idols. Elsewhere they are the foreign nations (e.g. Isa. 41: 1) or Israel herself (e.g. Isa. 50: 1). The summoning of witnesses at the beginning of these passages (including heaven and earth, e.g. Isa. 1: 2) and the legal background, have suggested to some that the origin of this literary type is to be found in a covenant renewal ceremony of some kind (cf. Deut. 31; Josh. 24). The frequency of similar expressions and imagery in the Psalms has added substance to the theory. But, as in the case of the oracles and Woe-utterances, the connection with an original setting in life has long ago been snapped, although the model is none the less effective for that. In any case specific references to the 'covenant' between God and Israel are rare in the prophetic literature, especially those parts of it (Isaiah, Amos) where the trial speeches are most frequent.

Various types of poem appear in the prophetic literature too. The dirge is one of the most effective. This was recited by mourners at a funeral (cf. Eccles. 12: 5), as in the case of David's lament over Saul ('How are the mighty fallen...' 2 Sam. 1: 19–27) and the book of Lamentations itself, which contains dirges composed when Jerusalem fell to the Babylonians. The prophet could employ this type of composition to great effect, as a biting comment on contemporary decadence, for example:

> How the faithful city
>   has become a harlot,
>   she that was full of justice!
> Righteous lodged in her,
>   but now murderers.   (Isa. 1: 21)

There is genuine compassion in the prophet's moving lament for fallen Moab (Isa. 16: 8–11), but the bitterly ironical poem on the death of the king of Babylon is more a taunt than a lament (Isa. 14: 14–20). For Amos the fate of Israel is sealed, and he sings a dirge over the country as if its people were already dead:

> Fallen, no more to rise,
>   is the virgin Israel;
> forsaken on her land,
>   with none to raise her up.   (Amos 5: 1–2)

Various types of hymn, drawn from the same sources as many of the Psalms, also occur quite regularly in the Prophets: hymns of thanksgiving for the birth of an heir to the throne, for example (e.g. Isa. 9: 2–7), or a general thanksgiving like Isaiah 12 (cf. 25: 1–5):

> You will say in that day:
> 'I will give thanks to thee, O Lord,

for though thou wast angry with me,
thy anger turned away,
and thou didst comfort me.
Behold, God is my salvation;
I will trust, and will not be afraid;
for the Lord God is my strength and my song,
and he has become my strength and my salvation.'
With joy you will draw water from the wells of salvation.

(Isa. 12: 1–3)

Hymns celebrating the victory of God and his enthronement as king are familiar from the Psalter (e.g. Pss. 93; 95–100). Isa. 52: 7–10 is a magnificent example from the Prophets:

How beautiful upon the mountains
are the feet of him who brings good tidings,
who publishes peace, who brings good tidings of good,
who publishes salvation,
who says to Zion, 'Your God reigns'.

Notice the characteristically Isaianic variation 'Your God reigns' for the usual 'The Lord reigns' (e.g. Pss. 93: 1; 97: 1; 99: 1), and the exquisite originality of the scene envisaged by the poet (cf. 63: 1–6).

The book of Amos contains three stanzas of a hymn in praise of the creator (4: 13; 5: 8, 9: 5–6). There are many others, ranging from hymns of praise no more than a verse long (e.g. Isa. 44: 23; 49: 13) to individual thanksgivings a whole chapter long (e.g. Jonah 2; Hab. 3). Whether the prophets to whom these compositions are attributed actually composed them or even recited them is a question to which we shall return later. The poignant lamentations and cries of dereliction in Jeremiah 11–20 are also loosely related to the Psalms and share with them some stereotyped features. But they have much in common with the more individualistic outpourings of the book of Job as well (see pp. 96, 103–4).

The prose narrative in the prophetic literature, both biographical and autobiographical, can also be analysed in terms of various literary types such as vision reports (including call narratives), symbolic act reports, and prophetic legends, such as those which we have discussed above.

Again, efforts to use this type of analysis to distinguish fact from fiction are likely to be fruitless. The persistence of such literary conventions underlines the lasting impression made by the phenomenon on succeeding generations of Israelites. Whatever they were actually like and whatever they actually said, the picture of these charismatic figures is a consistent and convincing one, from the earliest biblical examples, and before them the texts from Mari and elsewhere, right down to the Second Temple period. This is to some extent a literary matter. The prophetic literature, which is virtually all that survives of the prophets, accurately represents people's reactions to the phenomenon and this perhaps means more to us than the phenomenon itself.

Editorial arrangement

We come now, finally, to the question of how this whole variety of distinct literary units came to be built up into the impressive structures in which they are now to be found. First of all, it is possible to recognize various simple editorial principles such as arranging material according to subject matter. The most obvious example is the principle of collecting 'oracles concerning the foreign nations' into one long unit as in Isaiah 13–23, Jeremiah 46–51, Ezekiel 25–32, and Amos 1–2. Another is the so-called 'catchword principle', whereby one prophecy is joined to another, originally unconnected to it, by means of a word or phrase at the end of the first and the beginning of the second. Isa. 1: 9, for example, concludes a poignant description of the desolation of Judah with an allusion to the cataclysmic destruction of Sodom and Gomorrah. Then verse 10 starts a new prophecy attacking the immorality of Judah's leaders with another allusion to Sodom and Gomorrah, but this time to the immorality associated with those notorious cities.

There is, however, ample evidence to show that something very much more sophisticated is going on in the editorial arrangement of the prophetic books. There is a good reason why the 'oracles concerning the foreign nations' are arranged as they are, for example. Amos 1-2 gives us the key. We must remember that the prophet is addressing Israel; the foreign nations would never hear the prophecies against them. The climax comes when he turns abruptly from the foreign nations (including Judah) to attack his own country Israel, not just in the stereotyped two-verse prophecies aimed at foreign nations, but in a devastating catalogue of Israel's evil deeds, followed by a terrifying prediction of the inevitable fate that awaits them. The rhetorical point of this arrangement is clear: if you think Damascus, Gaza, Tyre, and the rest should suffer for their crimes how much more culpable are you, O Israel, whom 'I brought up out of the land of Egypt, and led you forty years in the wilderness, and gave you the land of the Amorites to possess . . .', says the Lord (2: 10).

The same point, writ large, is evident in the Isaiah collection too (13-23). After eleven colourful chapters on the nations of the world, their crimes, their punishment, in particular in relation to Jerusalem and Judah, and a spectacular vision of the judgement of the whole world (24-7), chapters 28-33 contain some of the prophet's longest and bitterest attacks on his own people, e.g. 'Woe to the proud crown of the drunkards of Ephraim . . .' (28: 1); 'Woe (RSV 'Ho') to Ariel, Ariel, the city where David encamped . . .' (29: 1); 'Woe to the rebellious children . . .' (30: 1). Is it merely coincidence that Ezekiel too, after his foreign policy collection (Ezek. 25-32), turns on his own people: 'Son of man, speak to your people . . .' (33: 2); '. . . prophesy against the shepherds of Israel . . .' (34: 2)? In the same way after the downfall of Babylon, vivid climax to Jeremiah's prophecies against the foreign nations (46-51), comes the fall of Jerusalem (52). The reader can hardly miss the chilling comparison.

Another editorial principle, however, softens the harshness of the last one and transforms judgement into hope. Again the book of Amos contains one of the best examples. Almost every word that Amos utters is a word of judgement and doom, and yet the last few verses of chapter 9 hold out a very real hope of rebuilding a new life beyond destruction. The effect of this 'happy ending' is to transform Amos from a prophet of doom to a prophet of hope. Looking back through his prophecies from such a standpoint, we find hope in phrases like 'Seek me and live' (5: 4; cf. 5: 14–15). Like Jonah's prophecy of doom proclaimed to the citizens of Nineveh (Jonah 3: 1–5), it can lead to repentance and forgiveness in the end, not destruction. The same principle is at work all over the prophetic literature, from short prophecies like the oracle concerning Egypt in Isaiah 19, which starts with devastating judgement (vv. 1–15) and ends with a unique blessing of Egypt, Assyria, and Israel (vv. 24–5), to longer units like some of the collections of doom-laden prophecies in Isaiah 1–12 which are 'capped' by a beautiful prophecy of hope. 4: 2–6, for example, comes after 2: 6–4: 1; 9: 1–7 after chapters 5–8; 11: 1–9 after chapter 10; and chapter 12 after chapters 1–11. It is likely that the magnificent series of prophecies of salvation beginning at Isaiah 34–5 is another example where the shafts of light that occasionally break through the darkness of the earlier chapters spread out into an almost continuous blaze of sunshine (see on 'Deutero-Isaiah' below, pp. 84–6).

Such an approach to the final form of the text of the prophetic literature raises a number of questions which we must tackle by way of conclusion. First, is there always a reason why one prophecy should follow another, or why some large unit, such as the foreign oracle collections, should be arranged in this way and not another? The answer is that of course there have been arbitrary, haphazard factors in the long process of transmission, from what the prophets actually said or saw on the first day of the sixth month 521 BC (Hag. 1: 1), or in the year that King Uzziah died (Isa. 6: 1), or the like, to the literature in which their words are now preserved. But we must always at least ask whether the arrangement is significant or effective.

Why for example has a predominantly prose account of events in the reign of Ahaz been inserted into the series of judgement prophecies beginning in Isaiah 5 and running on into chapters 9–10 (note the refrain in 5: 25; 9: 12, 17, 21; 10: 4)? The same thing occurs later in the book where a prose account of events in the reign of Hezekiah (36–9) has been inserted between the prophecies of salvation which begin in chapter 34 and run on through 40–55 and beyond. In both cases the purpose of this arrangement is clear: the inserted narrative adds concrete illustrations from the legends of Jerusalem and her royal house. The first shows what the faithlessness and disobedience of the people and their king, faced by a comparatively minor military crisis, led to. In the second the miraculous deliverance of Jerusalem from the Assyrian hosts and the recovery of the king from illness, not to mention the spectacular solar miracle performed by the prophet (38: 7 ff.), prove what kind of a God the Lord of hosts is:

> Say to those who are of a fearful heart,
> 'Be strong, fear not!
> Behold, your God
>   will come with vengeance,
> with the recompense of God.
>   He will come and save you'.   (35: 4)
>
> Behold, the Lord God comes with might . . .   (40: 10)

Between these passages come some legendary examples of how he does it.

The other question to be faced before we leave the literary aspects of biblical prophecy is: who was responsible for such editorial arrangement? The prophet himself? A later redactor? In some cases the answer is a relatively simple one. The book of Jeremiah was clearly composed in the same school as the so-called Deuteronomic history (Joshua–Kings) and can therefore be fairly confidently dated to the period of the Babylonian Exile, one generation at most after Jeremiah's ministry. One need only compare some of the prose sermons in chapters 7, 16, 17: 19–27 and elsewhere with the early chapters of Deuteronomy, the speeches and prayers of Samuel (1 Sam. 12), David (2 Sam. 7), and Solomon (1 Kgs. 8), or the narratives in Judges 2–3, 2 Kings 23, and the like, to recognize what a thoroughly Deuteronomic work the book of Jeremiah is. Prophecies uttered in the northern kingdom, like those of Amos and Hosea, were collected and edited by a Judaean hand, perhaps originally in the days of Hezekiah (cf. Prov. 25: 1). One may also detect in those books and elsewhere the influence of the Babylonian Exile, a time when prophecies of judgement on Jerusalem seemed to have been fulfilled, and the believing community looked beyond present despondency to happier times in the future (cf. Amos 9: 11–15). The Deuteronomic history itself contains such glimmerings of hope (e.g. Judg. 2: 18; 3: 9, 15; 2 Kgs. 25: 27–30), and some would suggest that the Judaean editor of Amos, Hosea, and other collections and the Deuteronomist are one and the same, although this is possibly too simple an identification.

It was certainly a long, cumulative process, and one thing is certain: if we devote our efforts exclusively to recovering the original words of the prophets, we will miss some of the individual voices that address us from later stages in that process, voices no less canonical and no less commanding for that. Both the original Amos and the later, fictitious character to whom the whole book in its present form was attributed have something to say (see p. 124).

3

The Message of the Prophets

IN view of the bewildering variety of material attributed to the prophets, it may seem misguided to attempt any comprehensive or systematic survey of their teaching. Yet it is not hard to identify common themes, particularly when we take into account the final shaping of the prophetic corpus. As we saw, the original words of the prophets, from different times and places in the ancient Near East, have been built up into the literary structures now before us, so that, as well as tracing the development of an idea from, let us say, eighth-century BC Samaria down to the time of Ezra and Nehemiah, it is also possible, and indeed desirable, to discuss the 'Prophets' as a whole. They are both a culmination of centuries of social and theological debate, and a part of the heritage from which Jewish and Christian communities have drawn their inspiration ever since. In the four short sections that follow we shall examine what seems to constitute the distinctive teaching attributable to this unique religious phenomenon. Where origins can be traced, these will be discussed, but our chief aim is to present each idea in its most developed form—the adult rather than the embryo.

In his famous maxim 'the Law is later than the Prophets', Julius Wellhausen wanted to suggest that the bulk of the Pentateuch was derived from the eighth-century prophets, not the other way round. Exactly what he believed existed before the prophets—a form of the Ten Commandments (Exod. 20: 2–17; Deut. 5: 6–21), or some other body of religious and ethical precepts such as the 'Book of Covenant' (Exod. 20: 23–23: 19) or the book of Proverbs, is not clear. Hos. 4: 2 can hardly be a reference to the Ten Commandments, and the familiar covenant language (e.g.

Deut. 29–31; Josh. 24; Jer. 11: 1–14; Ps. 78: 10, 37) is conspicuous by its almost total absence from the eighth-century prophets. Hos. 8: 1 is a rare exception. But one thing is certain. Their influence may not have been felt in ancient Israel much before the later parts of the Pentateuch, as Wellhausen argued. The image of the lonely prophet 'despised and rejected by men' (Isa. 53: 3; cf. 1 Kgs. 19: 10; Jer. 15: 15–18; 20: 7–18; Luke 13: 31–5) is good evidence for that. But this does not affect the importance of their ultimate contribution to the religious and ethical teaching of the Bible and, through Judaism and Christianity, to the world.

Social Justice

It is unlikely that the eighth-century prophets were the first to call for social justice in Israel. The legends about Samuel (e.g. 1 Sam. 15: 22–3), Nathan (2 Sam. 12: 1–15), and Elijah (1 Kgs. 21), for example, need not be wholly fictitious. But the historical fact that their words survive within such relatively extensive collections as the books that now bear the names of Amos, Hosea, Isaiah, and Micah witnesses to their unique impact. There were other factors no doubt involved in the eventual recording and transmission of their teaching: the apparent fulfilment of their predictions that Israel would be punished by enemy invasion, for example, when the Assyrian invasions in the last decades of the century took place. But few would wish to deny that many of those bitter attacks were actually delivered in the affluent years of the reigns of Jeroboam II in Samaria and Uzziah, Ahaz, and Hezekiah in Jerusalem, as the text says (Isa. 1: 1; Hos. 1: 1; Amos 1: 1, Mic. 1: 1).

Prominent among the prophet's demands is justice (Hebrew *mishpat*). It is the first of Micah's three virtues: 'to do justice, and to love kindness, and to walk humbly with your God' (Mic. 6: 8). Amos begins by comparing the social injustices in Israel (2: 6 ff.) with, among other things, the atrocities of the Ammonites (1: 13), and appeals for a revolutionary shift of emphasis towards justice and away from ritualism:

Take away from me the noise of your songs;
    to the melody of your harps I will not listen.
But let justice roll down like waters,
    and righteousness like an everflowing stream.

(5: 23-4)

Isaiah similarly links his attack on the sacrificial system at the Temple in Jerusalem (1: 10-14) with an appeal for justice (16-20). Verse 15, which links the two sections, graphically elucidates the reason for God's rejection of Israel's worship: 'your hands are full of blood'. If we envisage prayers with hands outstretched to God (cf. 1 Kgs. 8: 2), then horrifying hypocrisy is placarded before us. It is not only the blood of sacrificial animals that has to be washed off, but the blood of the innocent victims of injustice and oppression as well (cf. 5: 7; 59: 3, 7; Mic. 7: 2):

Wash yourselves; make yourselves clean;
    remove the evil of your doings
    from before my eyes;
    cease to do evil,
    learn to do good;
seek justice,
    correct oppression;
    defend the fatherless,
    plead for the widow.

(vv. 16-17)

It is this indissoluble link between ritual and ethical standards that the prophets tried to force their contemporaries to accept. Sacrifice without justice is worthless; and justice for the prophets means protection of the underprivileged members of society (Isa. 1: 17; Amos 4: 1; 5: 10 ff.; 8: 4 ff.; Jer. 7: 5 ff.; Ezek. 34).

The word 'righteousness' (Hebrew *zedek* or *zedakah*) often occurs alongside 'justice' as in the quotation from Amos 5 above. Isa. 5: 7 is another example: 'and he looked for justice (*mishpat*), but behold, bloodshed (*mispah*); for righteousness (*zedakah*), but behold, a cry (*ze'akah*)'. In Proverbs and Psalms it is extremely common in the general sense of 'innocence' or 'integrity'. But the two words are not the same. 'Righteousness' covers the idea of a 'righteous act on behalf of the oppressed', and thus 'salvation, victory', as well as 'justice' as an abstract concept. It is the word translated 'triumphs' in the Song of Deborah (Judg. 5: 11) and elsewhere 'victory' (e.g. Isa. 41: 2), 'deliverance' (e.g. Isa. 51: 5), or the like (cf. Zech. 9: 9). The 'righteous' God is not only one who demands strict justice, therefore, but one who saves and rescues (e.g. Isa. 45: 21). His people are obliged to 'act righteously' on behalf of the widow, the orphan, and the stranger too. The term *zedek* had peculiar associations with Jerusalem, as we can tell from typically Jerusalemite names like Melchizedek, Adonizedek, Zedekiah, Zadok, and Zadokite which all contain the root-letters of the Hebrew word for 'righteousness'. It occurs very much more frequently in the Judaean Prophets and the Psalms than anywhere else (Proverbs excepted). Jerusalem is known as 'the city of righteousness' (Isa. 1: 26; cf. 19: 18 LXX), and her priests descended from Zadok (1 Chr. 6: 12; 24: 3; Ezek. 40: 46), 'after the order of Melchizedek' (Ps. 110: 4; Heb. 7). The Qumran sect apparently called themselves 'sons of Zadok' (i.e. Zadokites), and the name 'Sadducee', applied to the Jerusalem hierarchy in the time of Christ, is derived from the same root.

Materialism constitutes one of the prophet's major concerns. There are many attacks on the idle rich: property-owners who 'join house to house' (Isa. 5: 8; Mic. 2: 2), squeezing out the peasants; men who live lives of drunkenness (Isa. 5: 11–12; 28: 1, 7–8, Joel 1: 5) and self-indulgence at the expense of the poor (Amos 6: 1–8); and women who demand all the fine clothes and jewellery that money can buy (Isa. 3: 6–23; cf. Amos 4: 1). Another form of materialism attacked by the prophets, especially Isaiah, is trusting 'in chariots because they are many, and in horsemen because they are very strong' (31: 1):

> Woe to those who go down to Egypt for help
>   and rely on horses . . .
> The Egyptians are men, and not God;
>   and their horses are flesh, and not spirit.
>
> (31: 1, 3; cf. 30: 7)

One of the most powerful and best-known expressions of this
view of transient and ineffectual human nature is in Isaiah 40:

> All flesh is grass,
>   and all its beauty is like the flower of the field . . .
> The grass withers, the flower fades,
>   but the word of our God will stand for ever.   (40: 6 ff.)

Jer. 17: 5–8 contains another beautiful and effective example,
in which the man who trusts in 'flesh' is compared to a shrub
barely able to survive in the desert, while the man who trusts in
the Lord is

> . . . like a tree planted by water,
>   that sends out its roots by the stream,
> and does not fear when heat comes,
>   for its leaves remain green,
> and is not anxious in the year of drought,
>   for it does not cease to bear fruit.   (cf. Ps. 1: 3)

The Hebrew word translated 'flesh' in these passages covers all
living creatures, human nature, and the material world in general.
Although it represents a bond between kinsmen (e.g. 2 Sam. 5: 1)
and between husband and wife (Gen. 2: 24), 'flesh' is totally
dependent upon God. God can destroy it (e.g. Gen. 6; Isa. 40: 7)
and also transform it (Joel 2: 28–9). By itself it is 'worthless and
empty' (Isa. 30: 7).

Closely related to materialism is idolatry, another target for the
prophets' criticism, especially Hosea's, for example:

> They made kings, but not through me.
>   They set up princes, but without my knowledge.
> With their silver and gold they made idols
>   for their own destruction.
> I have spurned your calf, O Samaria.
>   My anger burns against them.
> How long will it be
>   till they are pure in Israel?

A workman made it;
    it is not God.
The calf of Samaria
    shall be broken to pieces.

(Hos. 8: 4 ff.)

Here again it is the contrast between flesh and spirit, the work of men's hands and the power of God, that is stressed. It may be that, in the days of Hosea, Canaanite idolatry was a real threat to Yahwism, but this is most unlikely. In fact, Hosea's contemporary Amos attacks orthodox Yahwism, as practised meticulously at Bethel and Gilgal (e.g. Amos 4: 4–5), very much more vehemently than idolatry to which there is only one reference (8: 14). It must be remembered that the words of the eighth-century prophets were originally for the most part addressed to the wealthy upper échelons of society (e.g. Hos. 5: 1 f.; Amos 4: 1 f.) whose ritual observance could not be faulted. What archaeological evidence there is for the worship of Canaanite deities like Baal and Astarte in the period, suggests that it existed only among the poor peasant majority, and the prophets, as their champions, turned a blind eye to it, concentrating instead on the flagrant injustices practised by their pious leaders.

It is possible, however, that the faithlessness which Hosea recognized in his people, their disloyalty to the Lord, their 'harlotry' (e.g. 4: 10; 6: 10, 17–19), should be understood as just one more example of devotion to material things. There is a good deal in Hosea too about trusting in Egypt and Assyria (e.g. 5: 13; 7: 11; 12: 1), warriors (e.g. 10: 13), fortified cities (8: 14), and wealth (12: 8), anything at all that can break the bond of love (3: 1; 6: 6; 11: 1 ff.) between God and his people. 'Idol', in other words, stands for any kind of man-made alternative to God, anything that people devote themselves to, put their trust in, or make sacrifices for. It is in the Babylonian chapters of Isaiah that this reaches its most developed form. Chapter 44: 9–20 ridicules the wasted craftsmanship of an idol-maker; chapter 46 contrasts the effort required to cart round effigies of Bel and Nebo, two Babylonian deities, 'loaded as burdens on weary beasts' (v. 1), with the untiring saving power of Yahweh:

> Hearken to me, O house of Jacob,
>   all the remnant of the house of Israel,
> who have been borne by me from your birth,
>   carried from the womb;
> even to your old age I am He,
>   and to grey hairs I will carry you;
> I have made, and I will bear;
>   I will carry and will save.   (46: 3–4)

It is in this context that explicit monotheism is uniquely and persistently stated: 'I am the Lord, and there is no other: besides me there is no god' (45: 5; cf. vv. 6, 14, 18, 21). Earlier demands to worship God (e.g. Exod. 20: 3; Deut. 5: 7) or to love him as though he were the only one (e.g. Deut. 6: 4; cf. S. of S. 6: 9) are not strictly monotheistic. In these chapters, other gods and any man-made alternatives to God—wealth, military power, political alignments, religious institutions—simply do not exist.

The God of the prophets

The God of the eighth-century prophets is the God who punishes injustice by intervening in history. In legal language, the sentence is pronounced by God as judge:

> Therefore thus says the Lord God:
> 'An adversary shall surround the land,
>   and bring down your defences from you,
>   and your strongholds shall be plundered'.   (Amos 3: 11)

In Isaiah the way God uses historical events is even clearer: 'Therefore, behold, the Lord is bringing up against them the waters of the River, mighty and many, the king of Assyria and all his glory . . .' (8: 7). Assyria is elsewhere described as the big stick with which God disciplines his people (10: 5). Prophets in the Babylonian period recognized God's hand in the fall of Jerusalem (e.g. Jer. 21: 1–10) and later in the appearance of one who would destroy Babylon, namely Cyrus, king of the Medes and Persians (e.g. Isa. 45: 1 ff.; Jer. 51). Of course it was nothing new that God should intervene in history:

> Did I not bring up Israel from the land of Egypt,
>   and the Philistines from Caphtor and the Syrians from Kir?
>   (Amos 9: 7; cf. 3: 1; Hos. 11: 1)

The Moabites saw their god's hand in historical events too, as the famous ninth-century BC Mesha inscription demonstrates: 'Omri was king of Israel and he humbled Moab for many days, for Chemosh was angry with his land ... And the king of Israel had built Jahaz and dwelt in it while fighting against me. But Chemosh drove him out before me' (lines 4–5, 18–19). Examples of this can be quoted from many nations ancient and modern. But what is so striking about the prophetic examples is their moral content. For the Moabites a defeat meant merely that their god Chemosh was angry: for the prophets it meant punishment of Israel by a just God. Warnings are couched in historical terms, e.g.:

> 'For behold, I will raise up against you a nation,
>   O house of Israel', says the Lord, the God of hosts;
> 'and they shall oppress you from the entrance of Hamath
>   to the Brook of the Arabah.'
>   (Amos 6: 14)

Disasters can be explained away as momentary instances of divine anger and so transformed into sources of comfort (e.g. Isa. 40: 1–2). They can even be averted by repentance (e.g. Jonah 3: 10; Amos 5: 15).

In this connection we must remember that what actually happened is always less important than what its moral and theological significance is. Thus the prophets make no distinction between events for which there was actual evidence for all to see, like the destruction of Shiloh (Jer. 7: 12; cf. Amos 6: 2), and events like the Exodus (Amos 9: 7) or the victory at the Red Sea (Isa. 51: 9–10), for which no such evidence survives. Historical investigations like those that monopolized biblical studies for so many years were unheard of. In fact, so distant from actual history are these traditions, that the same language can be applied both to what God did in Israel's history and to what he did at creation. Thus God is termed 'creator of Israel' (e.g. Isa. 43: 1 ff.), and the myth of Yahweh's defeat of the primeval dragon of the deep is combined with the Red Sea victory in such a way as to 'historicize' the creation myth (cf. Pss. 89: 9–11; 93: 3–4). At the same time the historical event is clothed with timeless religious significance:

> Awake, awake, put on strength,
> O arm of the Lord;
> awake, as in days of old,
> the generations of long ago.
> Was it not thou that didst cut Rahab in pieces,
> that didst pierce the dragon?
> Was it not thou that didst dry up the sea,
> the waters of the great deep;
> that didst make the depths of the sea a way
> for the redeemed to pass over?
> (Isa. 51: 9–10)

'Rahab' is elsewhere identified with Egypt (Ps. 87: 4; Isa. 30: 7, RSV, NEB, JB) and the 'sea' with the Red Sea (Ps. 74: 13).

Later tradition carries the process farther. Thus medieval Jewish commentators recognize in Isa. 27: 1 references to the world powers Assyria, Egypt, and Tyre, although we know, both from the Ugaritic literature and from other biblical examples (e.g. Job 3: 8; 41; cf. Rev. 20: 2–3), that God's victory over 'Leviathan the fleeing serpent, Leviathan the twisting serpent and . . . the dragon that is in the sea' transcends history and belongs to creation mythology.

Although both in ancient Israel and in later biblical interpretation history thus takes pride of place, it is not correct to assume that the creation myths are 'late' or unimportant. In addition to passages, such as those we have been considering, where creation mythology is historicized, God the creator of heaven and earth plays another role in the language of the prophets. Amos 5 contains one of the most telling examples, where, sandwiched between two typical attacks on those who 'turn justice to wormwood (v. 7) and 'trample upon the poor' (vv. 10–11), this exquisite verse in praise of the creator appears:

> He who made the Pleiades and Orion,
>   and turns deep darkness into the morning,
>   and darkens the day into night,
> who calls for the waters of the sea,
>   and pours them out upon the surface of the earth,
> the Lord is his name.   (v. 8)

Whether we are to attribute this juxtaposition to Amos himself or a later redactor, and whether the next verse is moralistic (RSV) or astronomical (NEB), the point is clear. The God who demands justice and righteousness in Israel is none other than the God who created heaven and earth and all mankind. In the words of the proverb: 'He who mocks the poor insults his Maker' (Prov. 17: 5; cf. 19: 17). An assault on even the humblest part of creation is an assault on the creator himself. In the more developed imagery of Isaiah 45:

> Woe to him who strives with his Maker,
>   an earthen vessel with the potter...
>   (45: 9; cf. 10: 15)

It is in this context, too, that we must understand those natural phenomena with which God punishes Israel: famine, drought, blight, plague, earthquake (e.g. Amos 4: 6–11; Hag. 1: 10–11; 2: 17), not to mention the Plagues in Egypt (Exod. 7–12). Divine intervention is by no means restricted to the movements of peoples and military engagements. The hand of God is recognizable in nature too. The God who can make 'the wilderness a pool of water' (e.g. Isa. 41: 17 ff.; chap. 35) is of course the God of the Exodus, but he is more than that. The creator of Israel (Isa. 43: 1, 15; 51: 13) is creator of heaven and earth as well (45: 19 ff.). This means that he can harness the terrifying forces of nature to punish (e.g. Gen. 7: 11–12) as well as to defend (e.g. Josh. 10: 11–12).

At a more profound level, it means that even though heaven and earth should pass away (e.g. Isa. 51: 6) there is a greater power:

> Lift up your eyes to the heavens,
>   and look at the earth beneath;
> for the heavens will vanish like smoke,
>   the earth will wear out like a garment,
>   and they who dwell in it will die like gnats;
> but my salvation will be for ever,
>   and my deliverance will never be ended.
>
> (Isa. 51: 6; cf. Ps. 46)

Such a power can create a new heaven and a new earth (e.g. Isa. 65: 17; 66: 22). This is a doctrine that speaks of our ultimate responsibility for what we do on earth, and at the same time one that brings hope to those whose whole world is breaking up around them. Even if, for example, Jerusalem is lying in ruins— 'our holy and beautiful house, where our fathers praised thee ... burned by fire' (Isa. 64: 11):

> ... Be glad and rejoice for ever
>   in that which I create;
> for behold, I create Jerusalem a rejoicing,
>   and her people a joy.
>
> (65: 18)

Another concept given new meaning in eighth-century prophecy is the holiness of God. Isaiah's vision reminds us, first of the unapproachable nature of God in all his terrifying holiness, familiar to us from the tradition that 'no man can see God and live' (Exod. 33: 20), and the disturbing story of Uzzah, destroyed for putting out his hand to support the ark of God (2 Sam. 6: 1–11). But what Isaiah discovers is that holiness has a moral dimension too: 'Woe is me! For I am lost; for I am a man of unclean lips, and I dwell in the midst of a people of unclean lips; for my eyes have seen the King, the Lord of hosts' (6: 5). His fear of God's holiness is due not to his knowledge of what can happen to someone who, like Uzzah, gets too near to holiness, but to the knowledge that he is a sinner and member of a sinful society. He realizes that no amount of technical, ritual knowledge can render him safe from the holiness of God. Such a God demands justice, righteousness, faith, loyalty; not ritual sacrifice, sabbaths, and festivals (see above pp. 43–5). The Holy One of Israel is an Isaianic expression, but the concept infuses the whole of the prophetic corpus. It was moral shortcomings that led to the destruction of Jerusalem in 586 BC (e.g. Jer. 52: 2–3) and it was to protect the new Jerusalem from moral and social impurities, not just from ritual ones, that Ezekiel's massive fortifications were built (42–3; cf. 45: 8–9). Here more than anywhere else we can see the profound effect of the prophetic teaching on Old Testament theology: the 'holiness' of God's people involves obedience, not only to laws of ritual purity (e.g. Lev. 11: 44–5; 20: 26; Deut. 14: 2, 21), but to commandments that demand higher moral and social standards from Israel than from any other nation (Deut. 26: 16–18; 28: 9 ff.; cf. Exod. 19: 6; Lev. 19: 2; Num. 15: 40). Predictably the prophet Isaiah expresses this most succinctly:

> But the Lord of hosts is exalted in justice,
> and the Holy God shows himself holy in righteousness.
>
> (5: 16)

Finally, we shall look briefly at the kind of relationship such a God enters into with his people. The emotive term 'choose', so common in Deuteronomic tradition (e.g. Deut. 4: 37; 7: 6, 7; 14: 2, etc.), does not occur in the Prophets before the Babylonian period (e.g. Isa. 44: 1–2; Ezek. 20: 5; Zech. 1: 17; 2: 16; 3: 2; cf. Isa. 14: 1). But the idea is certainly there before then, e.g. 'You only have I known of all the families of the earth' (Amos 3: 2). In this famous line the verb 'know' comes very close to 'choose' (cf. Hos. 11: 12). The widespread view that the word means something more intimate than that, because of its euphemistic use in some contexts for sexual intercourse (e.g. Gen. 4: 1), is unconvincing; but the idea that God 'knew' Israel, in the sense of 'take cognizance of, notice, recognize' (cf. Isa. 1: 3), with reference to the Exodus (Amos 9: 7; Mic. 6: 4–5; Hos. 2: 14–15) or possibly the patriarchal traditions (e.g. Hos. 12), is none the less effective for that.

More explicit, and therefore more striking, is Hosea's application of the language of love and marriage to God's relationship with Israel, e.g. 'And the Lord said to me, "Go again, love a woman who is beloved of a paramour and is an adulteress; even as the Lord loves the people of Israel, though they turn to other gods and love cakes of raisins"' (Hos. 3: 1).

It is not important whether or not Hosea chapters 1–3 are biographical in whole or in part—that cannot be established one way or the other. The author wishes us to compare God's unfailing love towards his people, in spite of their unfaithfulness, to a man's love for his wife, however disloyal and cruel to him she may be. Although those chapters have a certain independence over against the rest of Hosea (they are partially in prose, for example, while the rest of the book is in verse), the themes of God's love and Israel's disloyalty run through the book from beginning to end:

> How can I give you up, O Ephraim!
>   How can I hand you over! ...
> My heart recoils within me,
>   my compassion grows warm and tender ...
>   (11: 8; cf. 6: 4; 11: 1–4; 14: 4)

Probably Hosea's insight played a part in the formation of Deuteronomic tradition, where love takes its place alongside fear, obedience, faith, worship, and the like in language about human responses to the divine initiative (e.g. Deut. 6: 15; 30: 15 ff.). The Babylonian chapters of Isaiah contain further developments, e.g. an 'everlasting love' for his wife (54: 4–8), the delight of a bridegroom over his bride (62: 5). We might add the gentle care of a shepherd for his flock (40: 11) and an architect's meticulous care of his plans (49: 16).

Of the few appearances in the Bible of the image of God as mother (cf. Deut. 32: 18; Ps. 131: 2), most occur in Isaiah. The special relationship that exists between a mother and her baby is compared to God's love for Zion (Isa. 49: 14 f.), and in the same context there may be an allusion to the fact that the Hebrew word for 'love, compassion' (vv. 13, 15) is etymologically related to a word for 'womb'. The related picture of God protecting Jerusalem 'like birds hovering' appears in Isaiah 31: 5 (cf. Gen. 1: 2; Exod. 19: 4; Deut. 32: 11; Matt. 23: 37; Luke 13: 34). In the final climactic chapter of the book God is represented first as a midwife assisting at Zion's labour (66: 7–9) and then as comforting her 'as a mother' (66: 13). Most striking of all, however, as an expression of the intensity of divine involvement in the human condition, is the image of God gasping and panting 'like a woman in labour' (42: 14).

Of all the prophets it is Jeremiah that speaks to us of the closest relationship of all. In the first place, in his so-called 'Confessions' in chapters 11–20 (see pp. 96–7), he himself reaches a new intimacy with his God. There are hints of this in the legends about Moses (Exod. 4: 10 ff.), Elijah (1 Kgs. 19: 4), and Jonah (Jonah 4), in some of the Psalms (e.g. 22), and in Job (e.g. 7, 10), but no prophet goes so far as Jeremiah (see p. 102). This intensely personal, inner turmoil, which transforms him, heals him (17: 14), restores him (15: 19), points to a new kind of relationship between God and his people. Chapter 31 contains a bewildering variety of material, not by any means all by Jeremiah. It is about return from exile, and new life in their own country. It is about God's love for wayward Ephraim 'chastened like an untrained calf' and penitent (vv. 18–19):

> Is Ephraim my dear son?
> Is he my darling child?
> For as often as I speak against him,
> I do remember him still.
> Therefore my heart yearns for him;
> I will surely have mercy on him, says the Lord.   (v. 20)

But what is new is the idea of a new covenant, which, like the betrothal in Hosea (2: 19–20) or the marriage in Isa. 50: 1 (cf. 54: 5 ff.), is unbreakable, and as fixed as the fixed order of sun, moon, and stars (vv. 35–6):

Behold, the days are coming, says the Lord, when I will make a new covenant with the house of Israel and the house of Judah, not like the covenant which I made with their fathers when I took them by the hand to bring them out of the land of Egypt, my covenant which they broke, though I was their husband, says the Lord. But this is the covenant which I will make with the house of Israel after those days, says the Lord: I will put my law within them, and I will write it upon their hearts; and I will be their God, and they shall be my people. And no longer shall each man teach his neighbour and each his brother, saying, 'Know the Lord,' for they shall all know me, from the least of them to the greatest, says the Lord. For I will forgive their iniquity, and I will remember their sin no more. (Jer. 31: 31–4)

The change of heart on which such a relationship depends is not new. We have seen it in Isaiah (1: 16–17; 30: 15), Amos (e.g. 5: 14–15), Hosea (e.g. 14: 1–3), and elsewhere. But here it is made possible by a divine initiative, exactly parallel to the Deuteronomic notion that God will 'circumcise your heart and the heart of your offspring, so that you will love the Lord your God with all your heart and with all your soul, that you may live' (Deut. 30: 6; cf. Jer. 4: 4; Ezek. 11: 19–20; 18: 31; 36: 26; 2 Cor. 3: 3). In these two chapters we come to the end of a line that began 'when Israel was a child . . .' (Hos. 11: 1). The story is told many times and in many forms—creeds (Josh. 24), parables (Isa. 5), acted parables (Jer. 18: 1–12), prophecies (Hos. 11), psalms (Ps. 105)—in them all God takes the initiative and man responds. In Jer. 31: 31–4 and in Deuteronomy 30, that response itself is initiated by God, and therein lies hope for his wayward people.

The city of David

The Zion traditions, including beliefs about the Davidic royal family, constitute the most highly developed and influential theme in biblical prophecy. Even for prophets like Hosea, Amos, and Ezekiel who may never have uttered a word in Jerusalem itself, the city and its Davidic dynasty play an important role. The only prophetic books in which there is no explicit reference to Zion or David or Judah, namely Daniel, Jonah, and Habakkuk, belong to a context where the centrality of Jerusalem, and in particular the temple (Dan. 11: 31, 45; Jonah 2: 7; Hab. 2: 20), was never in doubt. In the case of Hosea and Amos it is likely that words originally addressed to the cities of the northern kingdom (Samaria, Bethel, Gilgal) were later adapted for a Judaean audience, either by the 'men of Hezekiah, king of Judah' (cf. Prov. 25: 1) soon after the fall of Samaria in 722 BC, or more likely under the same conditions that led to the composition of a Judaean 'history of Israel' from Moses to Jehoiachin (Deut.–Kings). There too legends of heroes and victories, prophets and kings, from the much stronger and larger northern kingdom, are built into a framework in which Judah and Jerusalem take pride of place (cf. Judg. 1: 1–21; 2 Sam. 5: 7; 2 Kgs. 17–19; 25: 27–30). Probably the addition of the Babylonian chapters to the book of Isaiah, where again Zion and Jerusalem are so prominent, comes from the same period, the mid-sixth century BC. Bearing in mind our preference for the adult rather than the embryo (p. 42), we shall be more concerned with the effect of these Judaean or Davidic additions, than with how they came to be there.

First, as an indication of the extraordinary prominence of the little city that was captured by David towards the beginning of the first millennium, let us look at the names and epithets that are attached to it. In addition to its regular name 'Jerusalem' (attested first in the Ebla texts *c.*2500 BC and nineteenth-century BC documents from Egypt), 'Zion', 'Mount Zion', and 'daughter of Zion' are the most frequent and probably the most emotive of all. 'Ariel' occurs only in Isaiah 29 as a name for Jerusalem: it looks like the Hebrew for 'lion of God', and is traditionally understood in this way. Josephus, for example, tells us that in his day it was a name given to the Temple because it looked like a lion—narrow at the back with a huge and imposing facade at the front. In verse 2 it apparently means 'altar-hearth' (cf. Ezek. 43: 15–16), or perhaps some kind of ghostly spirit (NEB; cf. v. 4). Also in Isaiah we meet the terms 'faithful city' (1: 21, 26; cf. Zech. 8: 3), 'city of righteousness' (1: 26), and 'the holy city' (48: 2; 52: 1; cf. 27: 13; 64: 11; Jer. 31: 23; Zech. 8: 3; Neh. 11: 1, 18), all of which have a part to play in the creation of a Jerusalem ideology. Finally there is the theological name given to the new Jerusalem in Ezekiel's vision (40–8): 'the Lord is there' (48: 35).

It is likely that, before the eighth-century prophets, and possibly even before David, there were hymns in praise of Jerusalem such as Psalms 46 and 48, and other expressions of faith in the special status of the city. One in particular recurs in various forms throughout the prophetic literature:

> For out of Zion shall go forth the law,
>   and the word of the Lord from Jerusalem.
>   (Isa. 2: 3; Mic. 4: 2)

In the dramatic account of the Assyrian siege of Jerusalem (Isa. 36–7) there is an obvious allusion to the same couplet: 'For out of Jerusalem shall go forth a remnant, and out of mount Zion a band of survivors' (37: 32).

The book of Amos begins with another example:

> The Lord roars from Zion,
>   and utters his voice from Jerusalem
>   (Amos 1: 2; cf. Joel 3: 16)

All three prophecies, one about light to the nations, one about victory, and one about judgement, are couched in the traditional poetry of Jerusalem.

Whatever the origin of some of these traditions, there is ample evidence in the prophetic literature that events in the lifetime of the prophets were influential in creating new imagery and beliefs about Jerusalem. The first chapter of the book of Isaiah, for example, in all probability contains a prophetic comment on the disasters of the year 701 BC when the Assyrian army under their king Sennacherib invaded Judah (cf. 2 Kgs. 18: 13–16):

> Your country lies desolate,
>   your cities are burned with fire;
> in your very presence
>   aliens devour your land;
>   it is desolate, as overthrown by aliens;
> And the daughter of Zion is left
>   like a booth in a vineyard,

> like a lodge in a cucumber field,
>   like a besieged city.
> If the Lord of hosts
>   had not left us a few survivors,
> we should have been like Sodom,
>   and become like Gomorrah.   (1: 7–9)

The terror that gripped the citizens of Jerusalem during that crisis can be felt in various other poems from that period (e.g. 5: 26–30; 10: 27–32; 29: 1–4). So can the relief which followed Sennacherib's departure. In the first place, Jerusalem survived; only just (1: 8–9), but she survived. This provided the starting-point for a legend, recorded in both 2 Kings and Isaiah, that 'the angel of the Lord went forth and slew 185,000 in the camp of the Assyrians' (2 Kgs, 19: 35; Isa. 37: 37; cf. 2 Chr. 32: 21). This transformation of near total disaster into miraculous victory is a reflection of a Jerusalem ideology fuelled from time to time by historical events, but founded on faith.

The Babylonian literature, composed in the shadow of the destruction of Jerusalem in 586 BC, contains many examples, thus:

> I am the Lord, who made all things . . .
> who says of Cyrus, 'He is my shepherd,
>   and he shall fulfil all my purpose';
> saying of Jerusalem 'She shall be built,'
>   and of the temple, 'Your foundation shall be laid.'
>   (Isa. 44: 24, 28; cf. Jer. 33: 16; Amos 9: 11–12,
>   Isa. 29: 5–8)

As in the case of the 701 escape, so the rebuilding of the Temple in 520–515 BC, no doubt at first a pale reflection of the original Temple, fired the imagination of the Jerusalem prophets and strengthened their faith in the transcendent role of the 'faithful city' (e.g. Hag. 2: 6–9; Zech. 8: 1–8). The rebuilding of the city under Nehemiah (Neh. 1–6) probably had some effect too. By then, Jerusalem had become a symbol, with enough momentum to carry it beyond subsequent crises—under Antiochus in 168 (cf.

Dan. 11: 31), Titus in AD 70, Hadrian in AD 135—and a foundation stone of Judaism and Christianity.

The survival of Jerusalem in 701 has another role to play, however, in many ways a more significant one. The scene in Isaiah 1 with which we began is a scene of bare survival: only a leap of faith can convert it into a sign of hope. But the prophet's intention was to describe the destruction of evil—a 'sinful nation, a people laden with iniquity' (v. 4)—so that a new Jerusalem can be built. Destruction is refinement (cf. Isa. 1: 22–25; 48: 10; Zech. 13: 9; Mal. 3: 2). This is the corollary of the idea that the Assyrians and the Babylonians were big sticks with which God wished to punish Jerusalem (e.g. Isa. 10: 5; cf. Jer. 21; Ezek. 22). The furnace of affliction (Isa. 48: 10; Deut. 4: 20; Ezek. 22: 18) is not an end in itself, but a means of purifying or refining impure metal, and what remains after the burning—the 'remnant' (Isa. 7: 3; 37: 31–2; Jer. 23: 3; 44: 28; Ezek. 11: 13)—will be a source of hope:

> For I will leave in the midst of you
> a people humble and lowly.
> They shall seek refuge in the name of the Lord.
> (Zeph. 3: 12; cf. Isa. 1: 21–6; Joel 2: 32)

A number of historical events have thus left their mark on the Jerusalem motif, but we must remember that our texts have developed a long way from those events. Furthermore, it is striking that events of some importance in the history of the city have apparently had little effect on the development of the Jerusalem traditions. Hekeziah's reformation (2 Kgs. 18: 1–8; cf. 2 Chr. 29–31), for example, is not mentioned in Isaiah, nor is that of Josiah (2 Kgs. 22–3; 2 Chr. 34–5) in the book of Jeremiah. Finally we must bear in mind the recurring fiction that the eighth-century prophets uttered words we know to have been composed in the Babylonian period or later: Amos foretold the rebuilding of Jerusalem (9: 11–12); Isaiah blessed Assyria and Egypt during continuing wars with the Assyrians and political disillusionment with Egypt (19: 24–5), and the like. To hear the voice of the prophets of Judah, we must see the history of Jerusalem alongside the history of the theological idea of Jerusalem.

Nowhere is this more important than in the case of King David, son of Jesse, born in Bethlehem, conqueror of the Jebusite city of Jerusalem, and founder of the royal dynasty which ruled it until the sixth century BC. The discrepancy between the David of 1 and 2 Samuel and the idealized David of 1 Chronicles and Psalms is obvious. In retrospect the achievements of David, in particular the stability and size of his kingdom, add up to some kind of golden age (cf. 1 Kgs. 4: 20–8), the fulfilment of a dream (cf. Gen. 15: 18–21). Thus, although critical of individual kings—e.g. Jeroboam (Amos 7: 10–11), Ahaz (Isa. 7), Hezekiah (Isa. 31; cf. 36: 6–7), Zedekiah (Jer. 21)—the prophets clung steadfastly to the vision of a better age in which Jerusalem would be ruled by a second David (Hos. 3: 5), a 'righteous branch' (Jer. 23: 5; cf. Zech. 3: 8; 6: 12), 'a shoot from the stump of Jesse' (Isa. 11: 1).

Such 'Messianic' prophecies are difficult to date, since they reflect a continuing timeless belief in God's power to save his people and the nations of the world, 'beginning from Jerusalem' (Luke 24: 47). Isaiah 9: 2–7, for example, preserves a famous dynastic hymn which may well be part of an early stock of Davidic tradition, possibly even going back before Isaiah, while the even better-known Messianic prophecy two chapters further on (11: 1–9), in which the vision of peace and justice is expanded to include the whole world, is certainly later. Probably, in addition to the age of David himself, the upsurge of national fervour in Judah in the age of Josiah (640–609), and the hopes surrounding the rebuilding of Jerusalem under Zerubbabel (cf. Haggai 2) and Nehemiah (cf. Neh. 12: 27–47) contributed something to the rich language and imagery of this part of the prophetic tradition. The crisis of the Babylonian Exile also influenced the idealizing of the Davidic hope (e.g. Ezek. 34: 20–4; cf. Jer. 23: 5–6).

The terms 'Messiah' and 'Messianic', ultimately derived from the Hebrew for 'anointed' (*mashiah*), are applied primarily to royal figures, and are thus almost interchangeable with 'David' and 'Davidic'. In Samuel and Kings 'the Lord's anointed' is regularly used of the Davidic king (e.g. 1 Sam. 26: 9); the same applies to the Psalms (e.g. Pss. 2: 2; 18: 50; 89: 51). Curiously enough the terms do not actually occur in the prophetic literature, where, as we have seen, explicit Davidic language is preferred—another sure sign of the predominance of the Jerusalem ideology in the prophets. In English, 'Messiah' is also used in the sense of a future saviour figure, whether Davidic or not, and whether actually described in the text as a 'Messiah' or not. It is natural, for instance, to describe the subject of Isa. 9: 2–7 as the 'Messiah', and both 9: 2–7 and 11: 1–9 are legitimately known as 'Messianic' prophecies.

One final motif derived from the city of David is the Temple. Throughout the prophetic literature it is regularly associated with hypocrisy, injustice, and self-deception: thus

I hate, I despise your feasts,
 and I take no delight in your solemn assemblies.
Even though you offer me your burnt offerings and cereal offerings,
 I will not accept them,
and the peace offerings of your fatted beasts
 I will not look upon.
Take away from me the noise of your songs;
 to the melody of your harps I will not listen.
But let justice roll down like waters,
 and righteousness like an everflowing stream.
    (Amos 5: 21–4; cf. Isa. 1: 11 ff.; Jer. 7: 8–11; Ezek. 8)

A very important theme which surfaces in many passages and greatly influences the later history of Judaism and Christianity is the suggestion that God's people can be happier and more obedient without a Temple. Both Amos and Jeremiah question whether all the elaborate Temple rituals belong to the essence of Yahwism (Amos 5: 25; Jer. 7: 22–3). In a passage probably composed at the very time when the Temple at Jerusalem was being rebuilt (*c*.520 BC), prophetic criticism of Temple ritual reaches its peak:

Thus says the Lord:
'Heaven is my throne
 and the earth is my footstool;
what is the house which you would build for me,
 and what is the place of my rest? . . .

He who slaughters an ox is like him who kills a man;. . . .
he who makes a memorial offering of frankincense, like him who
blesses an idol.
These have chosen their own ways,
and their soul delights in their abominations. . . .

(Isa. 66: 1, 3)

The idea appears also in the David narrative (e.g. 2 Sam. 7: 5) and
in several other passages expressing a kind of nostalgia for the
innocence of the wilderness:

I remember the devotion of your youth,
your love as a bride,
how you followed me in the wilderness,
in a land not sown.
(Jer. 2: 2; cf. Hos. 2: 14–15; 9: 10 ff.)

When the Temple was destroyed, there were prophecies that it
would be rebuilt (e.g. Isa. 44: 28); but these are rare. The Temple
is conspicuous by its absence from many prophecies of hope, even
those in which the new Jerusalem is described (e.g. Isa. 2: 2–4; 4:
2–6; 26: 1–6; 65: 17–25; Jer. 31: 23–40; Amos 9: 11–15; Zech.
9: 9–11). Ezekiel's spectacular prophecy (40–8) hardly envisaged
actual buildings, and even Haggai and Zechariah, although
apparently present at the inauguration of the Second Temple at
Jerusalem (Ezr. 5), look beyond the stones of the new building to
spiritual realities which transcend them (cf. Hag. 2: 8–9; 21–2;
Zech. 1–8). The line from there to the vision of John of Patmos,
where the new Jerusalem has no temple in it, 'for its temple is the
Lord God the Almighty and the Lamb' (Rev. 21: 22), and to
the celebrated saying of Rabban Yochanan ben Zakkai over the
destruction of the Second Temple in AD 70, is a direct one: 'My
son, be not aggrieved. We have another atonement as effective as
this. And what is it? It is acts of loving kindness, as it is said, "For
I desire mercy and not sacrifice" (Hos. 6: 6).'
The political institutions of Jerusalem (the king, the city)
became central elements in prophetic idealism; the religious
institutions (the Temple, the ritual, the priests) never did. Hopes

centring in a prophet like Moses (Deut. 18: 18), and a great High Priest like Melchizedek (Ps. 110; Heb. 7) do occur in biblical tradition; but in the prophetic literature, the Davidic 'Messiah' ruling in Jerusalem takes pride of place.

The Day of the Lord

In this section we shall look at passages in which the prophets prepare us for the unexpected. Nowhere is this more brilliantly expressed than in the Babylonian chapters of the book of Isaiah, e.g.:

> Remember not the former things,
>   nor consider the things of old.
> Behold, I am doing a new thing;
>   now it springs forth, do you not perceive it?
>   (Isa. 43: 18–19; cf. 48: 6–7; 52: 15; 65: 17)

But we begin with Amos, and the new interpretation of the 'Day of the Lord' that he presents. Although this appears to be the earliest reference to the idea, it is likely that it was already an established tradition in his day, and his understanding of it therefore all the more revolutionary:

> Woe to you who desire the day of the Lord!
>   Why would you have the day of the Lord?
> It is darkness, and not light;
>   as if a man fled from a lion,
>   and a bear met him;
> or went into a house and leaned with his hand against the wall,
>   and a serpent bit him.
> Is not the day of the Lord darkness, and not light,
>   and gloom with no brightness in it?
>
>   (Amos 5: 18–20)

More detailed descriptions appear in later prophets (e.g. Joel; Zeph. 1; Obad. 15–21; Jer. 46; Ezek. 7: 10; 30: 1–5).

The oracle against Babylon in Isaiah 13 is the most elaborate. The picture is always one of terror on the part of people confronted by Yahweh: bloodcurdling images are taken from war (e.g. Isa. 13: 15–16), ritual sacrifices (e.g. Jer. 46: 10; Zeph. 1: 7 ff.; Isa. 34: 6), weird astronomical phenomena (e.g. Joel 2: 10, 30–4), and the like. God is 'cruel' and has come to punish the wicked. No one will escape except 'those who call upon the name of the Lord' (Joel 2: 32–3; cf. Zech. 14).

There has been much discussion about the origin of this concept. Some trace it to an ancient 'Holy War' ideology, thinking of 'the day of Midian' (Isa. 9: 4) and Deuteronomic instruction on war (Deut. 20). The spectacular role played by the elements and Yahweh himself in the legends of Israel's battles (e.g. Exod. 14–15, Josh. 10: 8–14; Judg. 5: 20) appears to confirm this view. Others compare the concept to myths about a struggle between God and some cosmic monster (e.g. Isa. 27: 1; 51: 9–10; Pss. 89: 9–10; 93; 74: 13 f.) and maintain that the 'Day of Yahweh' refers to the festival of Yahweh's enthronement. Probably both contexts, historical and liturgical, have influenced the prophets' language and imagery.

What is important is to see that, in using this concept, the prophets are predicting God's ultimate victory over injustice and oppression. These colourful passages are statements of faith in God's power to overcome evil. Whether derived from the battles described in Exodus and Joshua or from the myth and ritual of Psalms, the 'Day of Yahweh' means the day when Yahweh conquers evil. Those who 'desire the day of the Lord' (Amos 5: 18) are therefore those who celebrate that victory at their feasts and solemn assemblies (Amos 5: 21) by singing hymns and remembering the victories of God and his people, and how his anger is turned against his enemies. If God's people are themselves guilty of injustice and oppression, then they are God's enemies and will be defeated and destroyed with the same finality as were the Egyptians and the Amorites, or Leviathan and Rahab. Amos' 'Woe to you who desire the day of the Lord . . .' is thus not very different from 'prepare to meet your God, O Israel!' in the previous chapter (4: 12).

The Day of the Lord can also be the inauguration of a wonderful new age, in which there will be no more wars (Isa. 2: 4; cf. 11: 6–9), and prosperity and security for ever (e.g. Amos 9: 13–15). Many of these passages are introduced by the demonstrative phrase 'in that day . . .', which serves to bring them into line with the rarer 'day of the Lord' passages and to build up a composite vision of the future which has had a profound influence on Jewish, Christian, and, more recently, Marxist thinking. The vocabulary of this vision—'a new Jerusalem', 'a land flowing with milk and honey', 'swords into ploughshares'—originally referred to better times ahead, perhaps associated with a change in political circumstances or the like. The 'Messianic' prophecies, associated with the start of a new reign, certainly did. But there are hints, even in some of the earliest examples, of something transcendent, to which the term eschatological may be applied. This means that the present age will come to an end; there is a complete break in history; and a new heaven and a new earth are brought into being (e.g. Isa. 65–6; Rev. 21–2). Phrases like 'In the latter days' (e.g. Isa. 2: 2 RSV), which originally meant no more than 'in the future', are associated later with ideas of 'the end' (e.g. Dan. 12: 4) or 'The last days' (Isa. 2: 2 AV).

4

The Prophets (I): Moses to Huldah

FROM a thematic survey of prophecy we move on to examine the prophets themselves. Generalizations are valuable, but biblical tradition has preserved stories about named prophets, together with a few unnamed 'men of God', sufficiently different from one another to be examined as individuals. In some instances, place and date of birth, parentage, and other biographical details are given. In others almost nothing is known of them apart from a name and what they are reported to have said. Our task is to collect what material there is on each one of them, set it against what we know of social, political, and religious conditions in ancient Israel, and hopefully reconstruct a convincing and consistent story of each individual's prophetic achievements. We shall not be concerned exclusively with what the prophets actually did or suffered, however, or with what they actually said. We must also take seriously how tradition represents them, fact or fiction; and we cannot always distinguish the one from the other since it is in that form that they have influenced believing communities, Jewish, Christian, and Muslim, long after their actual achievements and original audiences had been forgotten.

In this chapter and the next, therefore, alongside occasional references to contemporary Assyrian or Babylonian or Egyptian documents, and to modern attempts at reconstructing how things actually were, we shall be quoting apocryphal legends and other late interpretations of the biblical material to fill out the pictures sketched in the Bible. In other words this is not going to be merely a history of prophecy in ancient Israel, but a distillation of prophetic legends, more sensitive to what the texts are saying and to what devout readers or listeners down the ages have heard them say than to what actually happened. It is the meaning of the texts we shall be concentrating on, and the way they have been understood and implemented in post-biblical times, not what Moses or Isaiah or Habakkuk actually said or did. The previous chapters speculated on what kind of people the prophets were and what kind of things they might have said, but we must accept that the individual personalities of the prophets, in all their richness and variety, are the creation of writers whose intention was not purely historical or annalistic. The prophets before us are spokesmen of God, miracle-workers, visionaries, who repeatedly break out of the constraints of normal historical narrative. If we concentrated exclusively on the question of separating fact from fiction, we would lose sight of the power and the glory of biblical prophecy. The characters will be discussed in order of appearance from Moses to Malachi.

The Five Books of Moses

'And there has not risen a prophet since in Israel like *Moses*, whom the Lord knew face to face . . .' (Deut. 34: 10–12). Moses is rarely described as a prophet in the Pentateuch, and in some respects he is atypical—in the stories of his infancy and early life, for example, and his role as lawgiver and religious leader. But he could hardly have been more vividly and more characteristically represented as a prophet. He was called like Amos from minding his sheep and, like Jeremiah, was immediately conscious of his inability to speak. He performed a long series of miracles, some like Elijah's to bring help to the needy, others like Isaiah's to prove his power to disbelievers. Like Isaiah and Ezekiel he was given a rare glimpse of God in all his glory, and brought into an even closer relationship with God than Jeremiah. He interceded for his people, not just occasionally like Amos (7: 2, 5) or Isaiah (6: 11), but all his life.

The Moses of our completed Pentateuch is a kind of 'Identikit' picture of the archetypal prophet. In all probability it is based on memories and experiences of actual prophets such as those recorded in Samuel, Kings, and the prophetic literature. This is not the place to tackle the complicated literary critical questions involved in separating out the various models of Moses contained in the Pentateuch—hero, lawgiver, prophet, and the like—to determine which is historical. Instead we shall select the Deuteronomic tradition just quoted, which draws together the various threads of Mosaic tradition, and base our discussion on it. After all, as we saw, it was this Deuteronomic tradition that moulded many of the prophetic narratives in Samuel, Kings, Jeremiah, and elsewhere, and its influence on later texts, where Moses appears with Samuel among the 'holy prophets' (Acts 3: 21–4), for example, and alongside Elijah in the Transfiguration (Matt. 17: 1–8; Mark 9: 2–8; Luke 9: 28–36), is unmistakable. Other traditions, such as the usual rabbinic title *moshe rabbenu* 'Moses our master, teacher', the Samaritan Messianic term *Taheb* 'restorer', which is modelled on Moses, and the universal belief that Moses was author of 'the book of the law', must not blind us to the rich and influential Deuteronomic Moses. For Hosea (12: 13) and the author of the apocryphal book of Wisdom (11), he is primarily a prophet.

In the first place, the Deuteronomic presentation of Moses transforms the Pentateuch from 'law' or 'teaching' into the vision of a prophet and, what is more, a vision concerning the future (cf. pp. 16–18). This is the effect of the author's striking emphasis on prediction in chapter 18, cited both by Peter (Acts 3: 22–3) and by Stephen (Acts 7: 37), and his moving account of Moses' death (Deut. 34). But we must not forget also the prophecies of doom and salvation contained in the Pentateuch, both those uttered by Moses himself (e.g. Deut. 4: 27–8; 18: 15, 17; 30: 1–10) and those placed on the lips of others (e.g. Gen. 49: 10–11; Num. 24: 17). An essential forward-looking dimension has thus been given to the five books of Moses which transports them out of ancient Israel and into the living communities of faith, Jewish, Samaritan, Christian, for whom Mosaic tradition is timeless and saving. Mosaic visions of the future appear also in Jubilees where the building of a new temple is foretold (Jub. 1: 27–8) and in the Temple Scroll from Qumran (one of the 'Dead Sea Scrolls') where, like Ezekiel (40–8), Moses is shown a vision of a new and perfect Temple.

The other essential ingredient of the Deuteronomic picture is Moses as a suffering servant. The idea that Moses should suffer for his people is to be found elsewhere in the Pentateuch, notably in Exod. 32: 32, where he offers to die for them. It could be argued that throughout his entire life he is torn between God's demands and his people's waywardness. But there is a special emphasis in Deuteronomic tradition on this aspect of his life. It is surely no coincidence that the book begins with a picture of Moses weighed down by his people's problems: 'I am not able alone to bear you ... How can I bear alone the weight and burden of you ... ?' (1: 9, 12). Later in the same chapter we are told that God was angry with Moses too, because of his people's sins (1: 37), and this is more than once quoted as the reason why Moses was not permitted to cross over into the promised land (3: 23–8; 4: 2–3).

The theme of the suffering prophet runs on into the stories of Elijah (1 Kgs. 19: 10; cf. Mark 9: 13; Jonah 4: 3, 8; Amos 7: 12; cf. 2: 12), Jeremiah (e.g. 11: 18–23; 20: 7–18; 36–45), and prophets in general (e.g. 2 Kgs. 17: 13–14; Jer. 7: 25–6; 29: 19; 44: 4; Dan. 9: 6; Matt. 13: 34). It is also probably the origin of the great Isaianic Suffering Servant theme (see p. 85), and at least one strand in the complicated Suffering Messiah tradition of early Judaism (e.g. Matt. 17: 12). The apocryphal 'Assumption of Moses' characteristically concentrates on the martyrdom of Eleazar and his seven sons (cf. 2 Macc. 6–7) rather than on Maccabean heroism. The modesty of Moses also became proverbial (cf. Num. 12: 3) and, according to Josephus, is the reason why his own account (Deut. 34) does not mention that God took him alive to heaven on account of his piety, like Enoch (Gen. 5: 24) and Elijah (2 Kgs. 2: 12). Incidentally, there is another explanation for the absence of any tomb or sepulchre (Deut. 34: 6): when he died, the archangel Michael fought with Satan for his body, and then hid it where no one could find it (cf. Jude 9).

Moses' sister *Miriam* is described as a prophet too (Exod. 15: 20 NRSV), and, in a rather bizarre tale, punished for challenging her brother's authority (Num. 12). She is remembered, however, with her two brothers, as a leader of Israel (Mic. 6: 4), and as a woman who, like the prophet Deborah celebrated the 'triumph of the Lord' (Exod. 15: 19–21; cf. Judg. 5). If her short song of victory can be interpreted as the basis of the much longer 'Song of

the Sea', now placed earlier in the chapter, then it was she who
first recognised the hand of God in the Red Sea events, just as her
namesake first recognised the risen Christ after the resurrection
(John 20: 14–16).

The only other prophet of note in the Pentateuch is *Balaam*, son
of Beor (Num. 22–4, 31: 8). By a fortunate chance his name
occurs on fragments of an Aramaic inscription from the wall of a
house excavated at Tell Deir Alla in Jordan, dated around 700 BC.
The text is badly broken but apparently begins: 'These are the
visions of Balaam the son of Beor, the man who was seer of
the gods. To him the gods came in the night ... spoke to Balaam
the son of Beor thus: "A blazing fire I want to kindle ..." And
Balaam got up next morning ... "Why do you weep?" And he
spoke to them: "Sit down and I will tell you what ... and see the
works of the gods."'

In biblical tradition he emerges as an unattractive character, a
mercenary soothsayer (Deut. 23: 4–5; Neh. 13: 2) who incited
Israel to immorality (Num. 31: 16; cf. 2 Pet. 2: 12–16; Rev. 2:
14), although in the earliest references (Num. 22–4) one can
detect a sense of awe and respect on the part of the author for
what God did 'by the hand of Balaam' (cf. Josh. 24: 10; Mic. 6: 5).
Later he is said to have died young (cf. Ps. 54: 23) and, like
Gehazi, the corrupt servant of Elisha, to have no share in the
world to come (Aboth 5: 19).

The legend begins in Num. 22–4 where Balaam, son of Beor,
is hired by the king of Moab to curse the people of Israel, as they
stand poised to overrun his land. Instead he proceeds to utter four
beautiful prophecies, e.g.:

> How fair are your tents, O Jacob,
>   your encampments, O Israel!
>   your encampments, O Israel!
> Like valleys that stretch afar,
>   like gardens beside a river,
> like aloes that the Lord has planted,
>   like cedar trees beside the waters   (Num. 24: 5–6)

Like Moses, Elijah, Jonah, Jeremiah, and others, Balaam is compelled to prophesy against his will and totally under God's control. 'All that the Lord tells me to do, that I must do' (23: 26; cf. 22: 19; 23: 3, 12; 24: 13). Like the ravens in the Elijah legend and the big fish in Jonah, a miraculous ass rescues Balaam from death at the hands of 'the angel of the Lord standing in the road, with a drawn sword' (22: 21–35). But Balaam is cruel to his ass and insensitive, and in later Jewish tradition 'Balaam the Wicked' is a kind of antetype to Moses and, still later, in some polemical texts, a contemptuous prototype of Jesus.

Dissociated from the characters who first uttered them, however, like some of the speeches of Job's discredited comforters, his prophecies have been gladly taken up by Jewish and Christian authors since early times (see p. 155).

The Former Prophets

There is sufficient unity of thought and structure in the books of Joshua, Judges, Samuel, and Kings to suggest that some overall editorial hand has been at work, and that one of his main interests was prophecy (see pp. 17–18). Leaving on one side the numerous unnamed prophets and 'men of God' (e.g. Judg. 6: 6–10), there are a dozen named prophets in the work, the first and the last of whom are the only two women, Deborah and Huldah.

Prophecy has almost no role to play in the books of Joshua and Judges. According to Judges 4, however, alone of all the judges, *Deborah* is described as a prophet by profession and her part in Israel's victory is to deliver the word of God to Israel's leader Barak. In this she is fulfilling the role of king's prophet: like Zedekiah in 1 Kings 22 she predicts victory (Judg. 4: 6–7), although unlike him what she says comes true (cf. Deut. 18: 21–2). She is at first disbelieved, like Cassandra and so many of the prophets (4: 8), and her second prophecy predicts that doubting Barak will be outshone in the battle-honours by a woman (v. 9). Her third intervention (v. 14) is to identify the most favourable moment for Barak to attack Sisera, the Canaanite leader, and all his chariots.

She is much more than a professional seer, however. According the celebrated 'Song of Deborah' in Judges 5, she represents the essence of Mosaic religion: she rouses the disunited tribes of Israel, reminds them of the Sinai events, and praises their leaders for offering themselves willingly. In short, her role is to raise the victory to a theological plane, e.g.:

> 'So perish all thine enemies, O Lord!
> But thy friends be like the sun as he rises in his might.'
> And the land had rest for forty years.
>
> (Judg. 5: 31)

In view of this she is given the title 'mother in Israel' (5: 7), which puts her on a par with priests so far as religious authority is concerned. Her prophecies were later applied to the pious heroes of the Maccabean crisis, where she is the inspiration for another 'mother in Israel' whose sons gladly gave their lives for their faith (2 Macc. 7). Alone of all the judges, she has the power needed to save Israel without any new experience of God's power: more like Balaam, or Samuel, or Elijah, than Gideon, Jephthah, Samson, and the rest.

Samuel belongs to the same category as Deborah, in that he is both prophet (1 Sam. 3: 20) and judge (7: 6, 15) in the days when 'there was no king in Israel; every man did what was right in his own eyes' (Judg. 21: 25). While Deborah appointed Barak to lead Israel against the Canaanites, Samuel is credited with appointing Saul and then David as 'the Lord's anointed', first kings of Israel. His place among the prophets is thus unique. Ecclesiasticus ranks him high (46: 13–20). His mother Hannah celebrated his birth by singing another 'Magnificat' (1 Sam. 2: 1–10; cf. Luke 1: 46–55). He is painted as a new Moses: a childhood story explains his name, for example (1: Sam. 1: 20; cf. Exod. 2: 10). He is associated with the celebration of the Passover (2 Chr. 35: 18) and given a Mosaic genealogy (1 Chr. 6: 13). His stern upholding of the essence of Yahwism against threats from inside Israel as well as from without (e.g. 1 Sam. 12: 6–25) makes the picture even more convincing. The original Samuel may well have had more in common with Balaam and Deborah, in his association with seers and sanctuaries, but thanks to the religious insights and literary creativity of the Deuteronomist and others who have contributed to the rich texture of 1 Samuel, he comes down to us as far more: as herald of the age of the prophets (cf. Acts 3: 24).

Samuel's more spectacular activities (cf. Ecclus. 46: 13–20)— his part in defeating the Philistines (1 Sam. 7), his control over thunder and rain (12: 18), his savage punishment of Agag (15), his anointing of Saul and David (10: 1; 16: 13)—should not obscure his prophetic message. More than any other prophet in Samuel and Kings, he speaks out against disobedience and corruption in a series of powerful speeches. The first prophecy, which constitutes his call, foretells disaster for the corrupt priests of Shiloh (3: 11–14), and is grotesquely fulfilled in the next chapter (4: 17–18). In his second full-length prophecy he warns his people of the danger inherent in having a king 'like all the nations' (1 Sam. 8: 5; cf. Deut. 17: 14–20), although in later prophecies he encourages Saul to accept the role of Israel's anointed 'prince' (10: 1–8). Then in his longest speech, after Saul is made king before the Lord at Gilgal, he repeats his stern warning: 'Only fear the Lord, and serve him faithfully with all your heart; for consider what great things he has done for you. But if you still do wickedly, you shall be swept away, both you and your king' (1 Sam. 12: 24–5). No such warning accompanies Samuel's other dynastic act, the anointing of David (1 Sam. 16: 13).

His memorable attack on ritualism, prompted by Saul's disobedience, is worthy of Isaiah or Amos and is quoted in Mark 12: 33 (cf. Matt. 12: 7):

> And Samuel said:
> 'Has the Lord as great delight in burnt offerings and sacrifices,
>   as in obeying the voice of the Lord?
> Behold, to obey is better than sacrifice,
>   and to hearken than the fat of rams.
> For rebellion is as the sin of divination,
>   and stubborness is as iniquity and idolatry.

Because you have rejected the word of the Lord,
  he has also rejected you from being king'.

(1 Sam. 15: 22–3)

Finally, the posthumous speech delivered through the medium at Endor (1 Sam. 28: 16–19) repeats his harsh ethical interpretation of Saul's sorry career. Like most of the words of Moses, these prophetic speeches are not of course the actual words of Samuel, but they add to the growing chorus of prophetic voices collected under the title the 'Former Prophets'.

The prophet *Gad*, 'David's seer' as he is called, was twice consulted by his employer: once when David was a fugitive from Saul (1 Sam. 22: 5) and once during the eerie happening at Jerusalem following the census (2 Sam. 24). His role in the second story is elaborately developed in 1 Chr. 21: 1–27, where he advises David to build an altar on what was to be the site of the Temple of Solomon. Along with Nathan he is also credited with responsibility for David's arrangements for the provision of music in the Temple (2 Chr. 29: 25) and, in later legend, identified as one of the unnamed prophets in Samuel's band (1 Sam. 19: 20).

Nathan is mentioned together with Gad in 2 Chr. 29: 25, and both appear as David's prophets. According to a later tradition (Ecclus. 47: 1), he is Samuel's successor in this role. Unlike Samuel, however, there is no story about his birth or early life. When he first appears, he is already David's chief spiritual adviser (2 Sam. 7). The occasion is David's proposal to build a temple at Jerusalem, and provides the context for the first fully developed Messianic prophecy in the Bible. Curiously ambivalent in his advice (like Samuel on kingship), Nathan at first encourages the king to do all that is in his heart (v. 3). Then, 'that same night the word of the Lord came to Nathan' forbidding it, and prophesying instead the birth of a son and heir, who will build the temple:

He shall build a house for my name, and I will establish the throne of his kingdom for ever. I will be his father, and he shall be my son. When he commits iniquity, I will chasten him with the rod of men, with the stripes of the sons of men; but I will not take my steadfast love from him, as I took it from Saul, whom I put away from before you. And your house and your kingdom shall be made sure for ever before me; your throne shall be established for ever. (vv. 13–16)

His later involvement in the circumstances of Solomon's birth is threefold. First he condemns David's treatment of Uriah the Hittite and his wife Bathsheba, Solomon's mother-to-be (2 Sam. 12; cf. Ps. 51). Secondly it is he who gives Solomon his 'religious' name Jedidiah 'beloved of the Lord' (v. 25; cf. Ps. 127: 2). Finally he is the one who initiates the plan to ensure that Solomon succeeds to the throne and joins Zadok the priest in anointing him king at the spring of Gihon (1 Kgs. 1). Nathan's powerful influence on contemporary affairs at court is further suggested by traditions that his sons were given positions of political, religious, and military power by Solomon, including 'king's friend' (1 Kgs. 4: 5), and that he wrote histories of the reigns of David (1 Chr. 29: 29) and Solomon (2 Chr. 9: 29).

Ahijah the Shilonite figures twice in Kings, delivering in both cases substantial dynastic prophecies to Jeroboam, king of the northern kingdom. In the first he foretells the schism on Solomon's death, dramatically represented by tearing his new cloak into twelve pieces, and the establishment of a royal house of Jeroboam in the north (1 Kgs. 11: 29–39). The second, a few chapters later, predicts the death of Jeroboam's royal heir, and the destruction of his kingdom (1 Kgs. 14: 1–18). Both are written for Judaean readers, and amount to prophecies of judgement on Solomon '. . . for he has forsaken me . . .' (1 Kgs. 11: 33), and on Jeroboam '. . . you have done evil . . .' (1 Kgs. 14: 9–10). In later Jewish tradition Ahijah becomes one of the seven saints whose long lives span the whole history of mankind: Adam, Methuselah, Shem, Jacob, Amram (father of Moses), Ahijah, and Elijah.

The story of *Elijah* is so thoroughly impregnated with the ideals and visions of his 'biographers' that the historical Elijah is less accessible to us than any other major prophet. Both in the Bible itself, and beyond it in Jewish, Christian, and Muslim tradition, Elijah the Tishbite is presented as the one who intervenes, unannounced, in times of crisis. Twice we are given glimpses into the private world of his communion with God: first, when he is miraculously fed by the ravens at the brook Cherith (1 Kgs. 17: 2–6), and later when, in the wilderness south of Beersheba, he is miraculously fed by an angel and confronted by God in that dramatic theophany of wind, earthquake, fire, and eerie silence (19: 1–18) (see p. 7). These two passages are enough to convince the reader of the source of Elijah's moral and spiritual strength. Elsewhere the stories tell of his appearance, like an angel of a *deus ex machina*, to kings or widows or servants, wherever he is needed to bring help or justice to those in distress.

This image of Elijah is epitomized by his first appearance on the scene (1 Kgs. 17: 1), and in the account of his final ascension to heaven with a 'chariot of fire and horses of fire ... [and] a whirlwind' (2 Kgs. 2: 11–12). Later tradition sees him as a *go'el* 'redeemer' as much as a prophet, and as the forerunner of the Messiah (Mal. 4: 5–6; cf. 3: 1–2).

The Mount Carmel story spectacularly illustrates his role as upholder of the Mosaic faith in a world dominated by idolatry (1 Kgs. 18). The story of Naboth's vineyard sets Elijah alongside Samuel, Nathan, Isaiah, and the others, as champion of social justice (21). The same concern for the welfare of the poor and needy is illustrated by legends of the miraculous 'widow's cruse' (17: 7–16) and the resurrection of her son from the dead (17–24). Discrepancies in style and content between the grotesque story of Ahaziah the son of Ahab (2 Kgs. 1: 1–18) and the other Elijah stories, and its morality (condemned incidentally by Jesus: Luke 9: 54–5), have been made much of by commentators. Fire from heaven, however, links it with the rest (cf. 18: 38; 19: 12; 2 Kgs. 1: 10–14; 2: 11), and is taken up in the early association of the prophet with the coming of the Day and the Lord 'burning like an oven ...' (Mal. 4: 1). The roots of this apocalyptic figure are firmly established already in Ecclesiasticus: 'The prophet Elijah arose like a fire ... His word blazed like a torch' (Ecclus. 48: 1).

In both Christian and Jewish tradition he is, after Moses, Abraham, and David, the most frequently mentioned biblical character. Most significant are those passages which prove that the belief in the return of Elijah, miracle-working prophet and forerunner, preaching repentance before the coming of the Messianic age, was well established in Judaism before Christ. Moses and Elijah appear together with Jesus at the Transfiguration, possibly as symbols of the Law and the Prophets, subservient now to Christ (Mark 9: 7; cf. Mal. 4: 4–5). Alternatively they may be precursors of the Messiah: Enoch and Elijah are more common in this role outside the Bible, but their appearance together in another apocalyptic passage (Rev. 11: 4–18) supports this view of the Transfiguration.

In Jewish legend, the record of the ascended Elijah's intervention in the affairs of men on behalf of justice and righteousness is unending. It begins in the Bible with his letter to Jehoram, king of Judah, predicting a hideous death for the king (2 Chr. 21: 11–20). Later come his involvement in the story of Esther where he is indentified with Harbona, one of the king's eunuchs (Esther 1: 10; 7: 9), and his identification as 'the bird of heaven' (Eccles. 10: 20) that brings protection in times of persecution. He also answers intellectual problems. The term Teyqu, used in rabbinic argumentation, is an abbreviation for the following: 'the Tishbite will solve difficulties and problems (when he comes)'—an admission of intellectual defeat! Finally, certain notable scholars claimed to live in the closest intellectual relationship with Elijah, like Jose ben Halafta (mid-second century AD), who was not afraid to criticize him for his bad temper, and the Baal Shem Tov (c. 1700–70), who had a lengthy meeting with the prophet.

Elisha became Elijah's disciple after the Horeb experience (1 Kgs. 19), although he is presented as different in almost every way from his spiritual master. In appearance he is bald (2 Kgs. 2: 23), wears ordinary clothes (2: 12), spends his life in towns and cities, is on good terms with kings, who address him as 'father' more than once (6: 21; 13: 14), and respected head of a guild of prophets (2: 15; 9: 1). Unlike his great master, he goes about healing and doing good in countless ways. The one spectacular exception, which could be the reason why he is remembered at all, was the brilliant intervention by which he masterminded the overthrow of Ahab and Jezebel, and all the House of Omri (2 Kgs. 9–10).

Few words are attributed to Elisha, but his actions speak volumes on the subject of justice and compassion. In one town he rescues pregnant women from having miscarriages (2 Kgs. 2: 19–22). He has the antidote for poisoned soup (4: 38–41), feeds a whole community with twenty barley loaves ('they ate, and had some left': 4: 42–4; cf. Matt. 14: 13–21), feeds a widow, then brings her son back from the dead, as Elijah did (4: 1–37), and horribly punishes his servant Gehazi for dishonestly obtaining money from Naaman (5: 20–7). The religious impact of his actions, though modestly expressed, is no less impressive than Elijah's. His miracle-working, for instance, convinces the king of Syria that 'there is no god in all the earth except in Israel' (5: 15).

Some argue that he is historically more convincing than Elijah. But it would be better to study him in the light of medieval lives of the saints, just as Elijah belongs more to the category of apocalyptic than to history. His example (unlike that of Elijah) is quoted with approval by Jesus (Luke 4: 27), as also by the rabbis, although he never gained the unique status that his master did.

Of the many other prophets that figure in Kings, the court prophets *Zedekiah* and *Micaiah ben Imlah* have already been discussed (pp. 11–13), as have some of the unnamed ones (p. 16). Several others are incorporated into the history of Israel and Judah. Jonah and Isaiah are two examples in Kings (2 Kgs. 14: 25–7; 18: 13–20: 19; cf. Isa. 36–9) and Jeremiah in Chronicles (2 Chr. 36: 21). *Shemaiah's* brief prophecies have an impact on the history of Jerusalem reminiscent of that of Jonah upon Nineveh (2 Chr. 12). *Azariah ben Oded*, like Haggai and Zechariah, inspired the king to undertake far-reaching religious reforms (2 Chron. 15: 1–18). His contemporary *Hanani* the seer was put in the stocks for prophesying against Asa because he 'relied on the king of Syria, and did not rely on the Lord your God' (2 Chr. 16: 7–10). Prophets are credited with having recorded the history of events at Jerusalem: Samuel, Nathan, and Gad (1 Chr. 29: 29); Ahijah the Shilonite and *Iddo* the Seer (2 Chr. 9: 29); and Shemaiah (2 Chr. 12: 15). His son *Jehu* soberly interprets contemporary history for the edification of Asa's northern neighbour Baasha, king of Israel (1 Kgs. 16: 1–17). These references add little to our overall picture of the biblical prophets; indeed in all probability they are modelled by the author on better-known examples discussed elsewhere. But they do illustrate the author's keen interest in the prophets, and the role of the word of God in the history of his people.

We come finally to *Huldah*, the wife of Shallum, whose role, parallel to that of Jeremiah (Jer. 52), is to predict the fall of Jerusalem and the premature death of the king. With characteristic (Deuteronomic) faith and vision, she interprets the one as judgement upon the place and the inhabitants, and the other as a sign of God's mercy on a repentant sinner:

But as to the king of Judah, who sent you to inquire of the Lord, thus shall you say to him, Thus says the lord, the God of Israel: Regarding the words which you have heard, because your heart was penitent, and you humbled yourself before the Lord, when you heard how I spoke against this place, and against its inhabitants, that they should become a desolation and a curse, and you have rent your clothes and wept before me, I also have heard you, says the Lord. Therefore, behold, I will gather you to your fathers, and you shall be gathered to your grave in peace, and your eyes shall not see all the evil which I will bring to this place! (2 Kgs. 22: 18–20)

This is the same unshakeable faith in God's love for wayward Jerusalem, that ensured that history ends, not with Jerusalem lying in ruins, but with the merciful release of the king of Judah from prison (2 Kgs. 25: 27–30) and the edict of Cyrus ordering the rebuilding of the Temple at Jerusalem (2 Chr. 36: 22–3):

Now in the first year of Cyrus king of Persia, that the word of the Lord by the mouth of Jeremiah might be accomplished, the Lord stirred up the spirit of Cyrus king of Persia so that he made a proclamation throughout all his kingdom and also put it in writing: 'Thus says Cyrus king of Persia, "The lord, the God of heaven, has given me all the kingdoms of the earth, and he has charged me to build him a house at Jerusalem, which is in Judah. Whoever is among you of all his people, may the Lord his God be with him. Let him go up." ' (cf. Ezra 1: 2–3)

Although it is actually in Isaiah 44 and 45 that the role of Cyrus, king of Persia is foretold, the book of Jeremiah does end with the same glimmer of hope after destruction as 2 Kings (Jer. 52: 31–4).

The Prophets (II): Isaiah, Jeremiah, and Ezekiel

OUR task in this section is a rather different one. In addition to a survey of the scanty biographical material recorded in the biblical and apocryphal stories about the prophets, we have literary questions to tackle concerning the date and authorship of the books that bear their names. The author of the book of Isaiah, for example, and his portrayal of the prophet will have to be discussed as well as what we know of the original eighth-century BC figure.

We shall also be looking at some of the more elaborate portraits of the prophets from later tradition. They represent the prophets as Jews and Christians have remembered them down the centuries, long after the original facts were forgotten, but they also frequently throw light on how the biblical texts are to be understood.

In the Greek canon, which is the basis of most modern English versions of the Bible (see p. 1), the 'Latter Prophets' constitute a 'prophetic Pentateuch' comprising four Major Prophets (Isaiah, Jeremiah, Ezekiel, and Daniel) and the 'book of the twelve' Minor Prophets (Hosea–Malachi). In the Hebrew Bible of Jewish tradition, on the other hand, there are only four 'Latter Prophets', that is three Major (Isaiah, Jeremiah, and Ezekiel) and the book of Twelve. Daniel belongs to the Writings. These four Latter Prophets then correspond to the four Former Prophets, Joshua, Judges, Samuel, and Kings (see pp. 72–81). The arrangement in both purports to be chronological: the Major Prophets lived in the eighth, seventh, and sixth centuries BC respectively (both Ezekiel and Daniel are set in the Babylonian period). The Twelve fall into three groups: the first six (Hosea–Micah) lived in the Assyrian period (eighth century BC), Nahum, Habakkuk, and Zephaniah witnessed the fall of Assyria's capital Nineveh in 612 BC, and Haggai, Zechariah, and Malachi belong to the period of the rebuilding of Jerusalem after the Exile. Modern literary critics and historians date the earliest texts to the eighth century BC, and the latest (e.g. parts of Joel and parts of Isaiah) probably to the fourth century BC.

Isaiah

Biographical details are few and far between, but they present us with a picture not dissimilar to what we know of the other eighth-century BC prophets Hosea, Amos, and Micah. Married with three children (7: 3, 14; 8: 3), it seems he lived all his life in Jerusalem in close association with the royal court. His considerable rhetorical skills, evident in his unparalleled use of word-play (e.g. 5: 7, 7: 9b), hyperbole (6: 10), poetic forms (e.g. 1: 21–6), allusions (e.g. 1: 9–10, 9: 4), and the like, show him to have been well educated. The accounts of his eccentric behaviour, such as his three years' walking about Jerusalem naked and barefoot 'as a sign against Egypt and Ethiopia' (20), and the sundial and healing miracles (38)—whatever actually happened—are evidence of the impact that he had on his contemporaries.

He was involved in all the main political and military events of his day, including the Syro-Ephraimite crises of 735–733 (7: 1–17), the proposal that Judah should enter into a coalition with Egypt in 705 BC (30: 1–5; 31: 1–5), and the Assyrian siege of Jerusalem in 701 BC. (Isa. 36–7). He shows considerable knowledge of international politics (e.g. 16, 19, 23), but his role was a religious and ethical one. He thought of Assyria as 'the rod of God's anger' (10: 5), for example, and the invasions as well-deserved punishment upon a land filled with injustice and corruption in high places (chaps. 1–5). He appealed for faith in God rather then political alliances with human powers (e.g. 7: 9; 30: 15). We can also assume that for him Jerusalem and the Davidic dynasty transcended the chances and changes of eighth-century history (9: 2–7) and provided a focal point for the whole sweep of

Isaianic tradition, sixty-six chapters long (cf. 1: 26; 26: 1–4; 52: 1–2; 65: 18).

Next to the Psalms, the book that bears Isaiah's name is the longest in the Bible, and in Christian tradition the most influential. It is an immensely rich book and, like the Pentateuch, spans four centuries at least, reflecting social, religious, and political conditions of many generations from the flowering of Israel's prophetic tradition in the eighth century BC to the fantastic world of apocalyptic after prophecy had died out in the fourth. Historical references include the death of King Uzziah in 736 BC (6: 1), Sennacherib's invasion of Judah in 701 BC (36–7), the destruction of Jerusalem in 586 BC (49: 19), the reign of Cyrus, king of the Medes and Persians (550–530) (45: 1), and the rebuilding of the Temple in 515 (66: 1–2). From a stylistic point of view too the book is far from homogeneous. Early passages like the 'Woe prophecies' in chapter 5 or the prophecies of judgement in chapter 3 may be compared with Amos and Hosea, while chapters 40–55 come stylistically closer to Jeremiah (sixth century); and chapters 24–7 can hardly be earlier than Joel and the later chapters of Zechariah, that is fourth century BC (see p. 9).

Yet the continuity from beginning to end, both literary and theological, is remarkable. Passages from the later chapters quote from earlier ones (e.g. 65: 24 quotes 11: 6–9); major themes such as God's action in history (7: 17; 29: 1–4; 45: 1 ff.), the concept of an individual saviour figure (9: 2–7; 11: 1–5; 32: 1; 42: 1–4; 52: 13–53: 12), the central role of Jerusalem/Zion, run right through the book. The distinctively Isaianic epithet for God, 'the Holy One of Israel', occurs thirty-one times in the book of Isaiah and only four times outside it. The book shows signs of editorial arrangement, which gives it a structural unity too. Thus chapter I functions as an introduction to the book as a whole. A progression is evident from the early chapters, which dwell on the sins of the people and the nature of divine judgement, to the later chapters, beginning 'Comfort, comfort my people' (40: 1), which take up the few glimpses of hope in the early parts of the book and present a rich and homogeneous anthology of hymns and salvation oracles. The last few chapters go still further, adding, to the earlier images of a new exodus and a rebuilt Jerusalem, the spectacular vision of a new heaven and a new earth (65: 17; 66: 22).

As for the view that chapters 40–55 are best studied as an independent unit by a different author, Second Isaiah or Deutero-Isaiah, there is plenty of evidence that these chapters are not by the eighth-century prophet but an anonymous exile living in sixth-century BC Babylon. There are references to Jerusalem in ruins (44: 28; 52: 9), life in Babylon (46: 1–2; 47: 1 ff.; 48: 20), Cyrus (560–530) (45: 1), and a Jewish colony at Syene in Egypt (49: 12). Assyria has no role to play at all in 'Deutero-Isaiah'. The theology of these chapters, for example their explicit monotheism (e.g. 45: 5, 6, 14, 18, 21, 22), ridicule of idols (e.g. 40: 19–20; 41: 6–7; 44: 9–20), handling of the Exodus theme (e.g. 43: 18–19; 52: 9–10; 52: 11–12), and vicarious suffering (53: 4 ff., 11–12), comes closer to Jeremiah and the Deuteronomist than to eighth-century prophecy. The same is true of the preference for 'our God' (e.g. 40: 1) rather than 'the Lord' or 'the Lord of hosts', and typically exilic terms for 'salvation' and 'creation' (e.g. 43: 15; 45: 15–17; 46: 13; 51: 15–16).

But it is one thing to identify a separate source: quite another to remove it completely from its present context. Right from the start chapter 40 emphasizes its continuity with earlier Isaianic tradition. The mysterious scene in which the prophet overhears the voice of God addressing his angels ('Comfort' is plural (cf. AV); and cannot be addressed to anyone else) is a repeat of the vision in chapter 6. In both the prophet interrupts the heavenly dialogue ('What shall I cry?') and receives his commission. The two glimpses into the heavenly court (cf. Job 1: 6 ff.; 1 Kgs. 22: 19 ff.) are intended to be taken together, the one explaining the other. It is also more than a coincidence that the celebrated 'Suffering Servant' poem in chapter 53 picks up the theme of the diseased body of Israel from chapter 1 (vv. 5–6).

Furthermore the stories of a miraculous turn in Jerusalem's fortunes (36–7), a healing miracle (38), and a prediction of the Babylonian Exile (39) constitute a most effective introduction to 'Deutero-Isaiah'. In any case the 'Babylonian chapters' include 34–5 and 13–14 as well. The case for separating chapters 40–55 from their context in the book of Isaiah is as weak as that for considering J or P only as independent literary units within the Pentateuch. The same is true of the 'Isaiah Apocalypse' (24–7). Whatever the case for separate authorship and date, it is an integral part of Isaianic tradition.

What has just been concluded about Deutero-Isaiah and the 'Isaiah Apocalypse', applies even more to the four so-called 'Servant Songs' (42: 1–4; 49: 1–6; 50: 4–9; 52: 13–53: 12). The view that these passages tell a story quite separate from the rest of 40–55 and were not written by Deutero-Isaiah goes back to the brilliant commentary on the book of Isaiah by Bernard Duhm (1892). Since then the debate has centred mainly on who the hero of the story is: Jehoiachin (released from prison in 560: 2 Kgs. 25: 27–30)? a new Moses, leader of the new exodus? Israel (cf. 49: 3)? the Messiah? the prophet himself? More recently, continuity between these passages and their contexts has been stressed. The picture of one who was 'despised and rejected by men' (53: 3) and later exalted (52: 13; 53: 12) is a common theme in Deutero-Isaiah:

> Fear not, you worm Jacob,
>   you men of Israel!
> I will help you, says the Lord;
>   your Redeemer is the Holy One of Israel.
> Behold, I will make of you a threshing sledge,
>   new, sharp, and having teeth;
> you shall thresh the mountains and crush them,
>   and you shall make the hills like chaff...
>   (Isa. 41: 14–15; cf. 40: 27–31)

The term 'my servant' occurs frequently outside these passages too (e.g. 41: 8; 42: 19; 43: 10; 44: 1; 45: 4). Moreover, there are wide discrepancies within the poems: the first can hardly be about the same person as the third or fourth. It would be better in view of these and other considerations to treat each passage as we come to it, in its own context, and try to understand what it is about, rather than who the servant is. The application of the poems to a particular person in history belongs to the history of interpretation (see p. 150).

The influence of Isaiah on later tradition, Jewish and Christian, has been inestimable, no doubt due for the most part to his close association with Jerusalem and the Davidic dynasty, which plays so important a part in the book. It is thus not surprising that tradition honoured him with two apocryphal legends: his Ascension, which tells of his journey through the seven heavens and how he beheld among other things the whole history of Jesus Christ; and his Martyrdom, which tells how the prophet was sawn in half for refusing to recant during the evil reign of Manasseh (2 Kgs. 21: 16) and thus joined the ranks of the martyrs remembered in the Epistle to the Hebrews (11: 37).

Isaiah 6

The chronological framework of the book of Isaiah (1: 1; 6: 1; 14: 28; 36: 1; cf. 2 Kgs. 15–20; 2 Chr. 26–32) asks us to imagine that the first five chapters contain prophecies delivered during the affluent reign of Uzziah (Azariah, 769–740), chapters 6: 1–14: 27 during the reign of Ahaz (734–714), and the rest during the reign of Hezekiah (714–696). The vision in chapter 6, however, reads like an entirely new experience in the life of the prophet, and is often regarded as an account of his call. It is certainly associated with the end of an era, and perhaps also with the arrival in Jerusalem of the first reports of the Assyrian invasions which were to devastate most of Israel and Judah.

The vision took place in 'the temple', but this may not be the Temple of Solomon at Jerusalem. The Temple plays a minor role in Isaianic tradition, apart from bitter attacks on the hypocrisy of those who worship there (e.g. 1: 10–17). This may rather be one of those moments when a prophet is admitted into the heavenly court (*hekal* can mean both 'temple' and 'palace') and overhears the voices of God and his attendants (cf. 1 Kgs. 22: 19–23; Jer. 23: 18–22; 2 Cor. 12: 1–4). At all events it is an awesome experience: exotic heavenly creatures, mysterious voices, earthquake, fire, smoke, and God himself, sitting in all his glory on a throne, 'high and lifted up'. The last phrase is repeated in 57: 15 and echoed in the description of the Servant of the Lord in 52: 13. The scene itself is alluded to in 40: 1–8, where once again the prophet overhears the heavenly voices, including that of God summoning his angels to 'comfort, comfort my people' (see p. 85).

The hymn sung by the seraphim (v. 3), known as the 'Sanctus' or 'Trisagion' in Christian liturgical tradition and the 'Kedushah' in Jewish tradition, contains the heart of Isaianic prophecy, rooted no doubt in the original insights of its founder, Isaiah of Jerusalem. It is, first, a kind of explanation of the almost exclusively Isaianic title of 'the Holy One of Israel' (see p. 84), stressing the terrifying power of Israel's God. The holiness of God can kill and maim: Uzziah was a conspicuous example (2 Chr. 26: 16–21). But Isaiah discovers here that it is not ritual purity that protects people from the Holy One of Israel, but moral purity. The fire that slew the sons of Aaron (Lev. 10: 1–3) and the innocent Uzzah (2 Sam. 6: 1–11) becomes a means of forgiveness to one who repents (v. 7) and judgement to the unclean (that is morally unclean) people he is living among (v. 5). The confrontation between the creator of heaven and earth and mere human beings is a common enough theme in the prophetic literature (see pp. 50–1). The distinctive contribution of Isaiah is his interpretation of holiness. In Isaianic idiom the phrases holy seed (6: 13), holy people (62: 12), holy city (48: 2; 52: 1), the holy way (35: 8), and the like take on a new and more challenging meaning.

The prophet's first message to his people after this vision is a prophecy of judgement, interrupted by a pathetic 'How long, O Lord?'. In the same way Amos pleaded with God to be lenient to his people (Amos 7: 2, 5), and Moses offered to die for them (Exod. 32: 32). But here, as in Jeremiah 7: 16 and elsewhere, the prophet's pleas go unheard. The people are beyond forgiveness, and the prophet's task is to tell them that there is no hope, no opportunity for repentance, no opportunity to 'turn and be healed' (v. 10). In the Gospels, the prophet's words are to separate the sheep from the goats, disciples who understand from the majority who do not (Matt. 13: 14–15; Mark 4: 12); but here only Isaiah is separated from his people. The rest are doomed. Notice how the impersonal and scornful 'this people' is preferred to the normal Isaianic 'my people' here (vv. 9–10).

The scene of desolation that will inevitably result is described in verses 11–13. Perhaps like 1: 7–9 the picture is coloured by the prophet's own experience of an Assyrian invasion or reports of one. At any rate the scene became all too familiar to the people of the region during the last decade of the eighth century BC and was interpreted as proof that the prophet's words were true (p. 40). This may well be one reason why the words of all the eighth-century prophets have been so extensively preserved.

The last verse in the chapter has been much discussed. The word translated 'stump' in the RSV ('substance' AV; 'sacred pole' NEB) was fastened on to by the Jerusalem hierarchy who found there, presumably after the terrible prophecy had been fulfilled, a glimpse of hope beyond disaster. The stump that remains standing is enough to give new life to the 'Righteous Branch' (4: 2; Jer. 23: 5) or 'the stem of Jesse' (11: 1). A Davidic king would emerge from the ruins to save his people. The Qumran community saw this verse in a different light (see p. 151).

The Isaiah Apocalypse

Isaiah 24–7 illustrates just how short a step it is from prophecy to apocalyptic. Here we find traditional prophetic themes in abundance, like the city, the mountain of the Lord, the vineyard, the return of the exiles, and so on, combined with visions of the end of the world, astronomical portents, an eschatological banquet, the last judgement, and the resurrection of the dead, in what has been called the 'Isaiah Apocalypse'. True apocalyptic, as represented by Revelation, Enoch, 2 Esdras, and the like, is more erudite and often contains more elaborate angelology, symbolic numbers, patterns in history, and above all some account of the mystical visions, journeys, and other experiences of the author. These are missing from Isaiah 24–7. Nevertheless, the bewildering concentration of cataclysmic images and unearthly visions makes the section unique in biblical prophecy.

Composed partly of earlier materials, it reached its present form probably in the fourth century BC, at about the same time as the book of Joel. Both authors were probably eyewitnesses of one or other of the spectacular eclipses of the sun which were total in Jerusalem during that period. The astronomical imagery of the time (e.g. Isa. 24: 23; Joel 2: 10, 31) was probably influenced by such phenomena.

In a way Isaiah 24–7 is a microcosm of the whole book. The progression from 'the city of chaos' in 24: 10 to the 'New Jerusalem' in 27: 12 echoes the progression from the hideous scenes of desolation in chapter 1 to the vision of a new Jerusalem in chapters 65–6. The cosmic imagery in 24: 17–20 alludes to primordial chaos as described in Genesis (e.g. 1: 2; 7: 11). It also contains an exciting alliteration: *paḥad . . . paḥat . . . paḥ* ('terror . . . pit . . . snare' v. 17).

Verses 21–3 come still closer to the world of apocalyptic ideas. They describe the final battle between Israel's God and the angelic representatives of the nations of the world (cf. Deut. 32: 8), collectively termed 'the host of heaven'. Dan. 10: 13 uses this way of interpreting history too. The stars are caught up in the battle (cf. Judg. 5: 20), and God's victory is celebrated, as in some of the Psalms (e.g. 89, 93, 95–100), with his enthronement. The chapter ends with a clear allusion to the extraordinary apocalyptic incident at Sinai (Exod. 24: 9–11).

The visions are punctuated by hymns and prayers, expressing the response of the faithful few to these cataclysmic events. The first of these (24: 12–16) contains two puzzling expressions, indications perhaps that in these chapters the author is breaking new ground. The first, translated 'in the east' (RSV), seems to mean literally 'in/with the fires'. The word occurs four times in Isaiah, always in the sense of 'fire' (31: 9; 44: 16; 57: 14; 50: 11). Here it is usually explained as a geographical term, 'in the tropics' (cf. AV) or 'in the east' (RSV, NEB, JB), but this is not totally convincing. Alternatively it could mean 'with fires', that is 'with beacons' to pass the news of victory over the sea from coastland to coastland. It is a chapter where we may legitimately expect to find original images, and this would be a most effective parallel to the second half of the verse:

> Therefore light beacons to give glory to the Lord,
> from coast to coast, to the name of the Lord.

The other problem is the phrase translated 'I pine away, I pine away!' (RSV) in verse 16. This interruption of the prophet is reminiscent of chapter 6 ('How long, O Lord?'), but also of apocalyptic passages like Dan. 10: 16. The plain meaning of the words, supported by Dan. 2: 19 (cf. 4: 9), is 'my mystery (*raz*) is with me' and, remembering that this 'apocalypse' bridges the gap between prophecy and early Judaism, we should probably prefer this to 'Enough, enough!' (JB), 'Villainy, villainy!' (NEB), and other ingenious proposals. Whether the speaker is the prophet, as the Hebrew text implies, or a divine voice, as the Jewish Targum (p. 150) suggests, is unclear, but the normal meaning of the word *raz* in a mysterious apocalyptic context must surely be preferred.

The eschatological banquet in chapter 25 highlights the awesome division between the sheep and the goats on the day of judgement (cf. Matt. 25: 31–46). While the wicked flounder helplessly in a cesspool (vv. 10–12), the poor and needy who trust in the Lord enjoy a banquet in the safety and splendour of the new Jerusalem high above them (vv. 6–9), The menu is brilliantly conjured up in two words, each repeated twice (v. 6): *shemanim* 'fat things', which include all sorts of meat, fruit, and vegetables, rich and filled with goodness; and *shemarim* 'dregs, lees', which suggests unrestrained drinking (cf. Ps. 75: 8) and the exquisite flavour and high alcoholic content of wine made from the lees (cf. Ezek. 39: 17–20).

The hymn in chapter 26 takes up the two major themes of the preceding chapter. First 'the strong city' where the righteous find 'perfect peace' (*shalom shalom*: v. 3) and security is contrasted with 'the lofty city' (v. 5), where the wicked once lived, now razed to the ground and trampled under the feet of the poor and needy. Then the resurrection of the dead is foretold:

> Thy dead shall live, their bodies shall arise.
>> O dwellers in the dust, awake and sing for joy!
> For thy dew is a dew of light,
>> and on the land of the shades thou wilt let it fall.   (v.19)

Like the vision of the valley of dry bones (Ezek. 37), this could refer to the resurrection of Israel from the ruins of exile, that is to say a national resurrection. But the Hebrew text actually has 'my body' in verse 19, a clear reference to individual resurrection. This accords so well with the radical new imagery of the rest of these chapters that, even if it is not original, we can recognize here the seeds of early Jewish eschatology.

Chapter 27 again draws on ancient ideas and images. The striking expression 'Leviathan the fleeing serpent, Leviathan the twisting serpent' in verse 1, for example, is attested almost word for word in the Ugaritic texts from fourteenth-century BC Syria, as is the myth of a divine victory over it (v. 1). The geographical terms in verse 12 allude to the borders of the Promised Land at its greatest under David and Solomon (e.g. Gen. 15: 18; 1 Kgs. 8: 65), and the great trumpet to the jubilee year when freedom was proclaimed throughout the land (Lev. 25: 10; cf. Isa. 61: 1–4; 58: 1). But the prophecy points towards a day of ultimate victory that transcends earlier hopes. It was natural that these symbols were related to later events in Jewish history, Leviathan to Assyria and the 'dragon that is in the sea' to the Romans. Rahab in parallel passages (e.g. 51: 9–10) was identified with Egypt (cf. 30: 7). The trumpet call, announcing liberty to the captives, will be heard, not just throughout the land (Lev. 25: 10), but as far away as Egypt and Assyria, where the 'year of the Lord's favour' (61: 1) will be proclaimed.

Isaiah 52: 13–53: 12

The last of the so-called 'Servant Songs' is in three parts. In the first and last the speaker is God, while the middle section (53: 1–11) is written in the first person plural, as though spoken by a chorus. The subject of the poem is suffering and release from suffering, expressed in a rich tapestry of images, including physical disease, social isolation, legal processes, ritual sacrifice, death, resurrection, and military victory. In form it is best understood as a communal hymn of thanksgiving for escape from suffering, like Psalms 115, 124, and 126, but the vicarious element is without parallel: it is the servant who suffers, but the chorus who celebrate release and victory.

The servant is introduced by God (as in 42: 1) and the happy ending of the story anticipated in language taken almost directly from 6: 1 (cf. also 57: 15):

> He shall be exalted and lifted up,
> and shall be very high   (52: 12)

From the very first words of the poem, we are led to expect something radically new and transcendent. The glory that is to be revealed in the life of the servant is compared to the glory of God himself. Verses 14 and 15 continue the theme by describing the unnerving effect he will have on kings and nations. His appearance is described as so hideously disfigured that, like Job (2: 12), he was unrecognizable: more like an animal than a human being (v. 14).

The word 'startle' (RSV) is based on an ingenious linguistic argument and gives a more conventional meaning. But the Hebrew word normally means 'sprinkle', in the leprosy ritual, for example (Lev. 14: 7), and in view of the consistently unconventional language and imagery of this passage, is by no means to be rejected. Ritual imagery appears later in the poem (e.g. 53: 4, 6, 7, 10), and would marvellously combine the theme of the leper, disfigured and cut off from society, with the idea that through his experience he will cleanse and liberate others. Note also the thematic link with 52: 11, the close of the preceding passage: 'Go out from the midst of her, purify yourselves ...'.

Chapter 53 begins with a change of speaker: the next section (vv. 1–11) is on the lips of a chorus who tell the story of the servant. The story is in two parts, each consisting of a description of the servant's plight and a theological interpretation of it beginning 'Surely he has borne our griefs ...' (v. 4) and 'Yet it was the will of the Lord to bruise him ...' (v. 10). The first part depicts the suffering as physical and social, like that of a leper, 'despised and rejected by men'. The Hebrew word for 'men' is an unusual form and connotes 'men of standing' (cf. Prov. 8: 4), stressing the social implications of the disease. The Hebrew words for 'sorrows' and 'griefs' (RSV) more commonly refer to physical suffering and, in view of what has been said above, 'sickness' and 'pain' (RSV margin) are to be preferred. The same applies in verse 10 below.

The chorus had thought the man was a normal victim of disease, 'stricken' and 'smitten by God' because of his sins, as Job's comforters did (e.g. Job 4: 7 ff.; 8: 20). But by a leap of faith, unique in the Prophets, they discover that he is no ordinary leper, but the servant of the Lord, and that through his innocent suffering they experience forgiveness of their sins and healing of their wounds (vv. 4–6). The nearest parallel to this language is to be found in the scapegoat ritual in Leviticus 16: 'The goat shall bear all their iniquities upon him . . .' (v. 22). But here and in verse 12 that language is applied to a human agent, and the process, described as 'an offering for sin' in verse 10, involves self-sacrifice. The word translated 'has laid on him' in verse 6 is the same as that translated 'made intercession' in verse 12, and expresses this idea in another way. The servant stands in our place, interceding for us, like Moses (Exod. 32: 32), and suffering the punishment that should be ours. The first person plural form in which this part of the poem is written has made it possible for believers in all generations, Jews and Christians, to share in this extraordinary experience.

The second part of the 'chorus' describes the suffering of the servant in legal terms (vv. 7–11). He was apparently arrested and put to death as a criminal, although guilty of no crime. The language recalls that of Jeremiah's 'Confessions' (e.g. 11: 19) and some of the Psalms (e.g. 7: 17), and again is intended to go beyond any actual experience. Death is often a symbol of extreme suffering (e.g. Ps. 18: 45; Isa. 38: 17), although here the added details of where he was buried—'with the wicked and with a rich man in his death' (v. 9)—seem to demand that we interpret this part of the story, like the rest of it, as unique and transcendent.

The language of the Hebrew text of verses 10–11, which contains the second theological interpretation of the servant's suffering, is difficult. This is no doubt partly because it attempts to say something radically new. 'If you consider his life as an offering for sin' (v. 10) (RSV 'when he makes himself' is an emended text) seems to ask the reader to contemplate the sheer magnitude of the servant's moral breakthrough.

In Hebrew verse 11 reads 'after the travail of his soul, he will see; he will be satisfied'. Psalm 17: 15 uses language so close that we must assume a semantic connection:

As for me *I shall see* your face in righteousness;
    when I awake, *I shall be satisfied* with beholding your form.

There is no need to add an object for the verb 'see' as is done in the Isaiah Scroll from Qumran ('he shall see light'; cf. NEB). It is also unnecessary to decide whether death and resurrection here were intended to be understood literally or not. The sense of ultimate victory over suffering is clear enough.

The verb rendered 'make many to be accounted righteous' occurs in this sense only here and in Dan. 12: 3, which confirms our impression that, as it stands, the Hebrew text of Isaiah 53 has eschatological associations whatever the original text may have intended.

The third part of the poem (v. 12) reverts once more to the direct words of God, who concludes by foretelling the ultimate triumph of his servant and, in strongly worded language, giving his own interpretation of the story:

> because he poured out his soul to death,
>> and was numbered with the transgressors;
> yet he bore the sin of many,
>> and made intercession for the transgressors.

Jeremiah

The book of Jeremiah raises similar problems of date and authorship to those in the book of Isaiah, but it spans a shorter period—two or three generations at the most—and contains far less variety of material. Moreover, the portrayal of Jeremiah, whatever its resemblance to the original prophet, is a fuller and more consistent one than that of Isaiah. The overall shape of the book is governed by a comprehensive prose narrative, written, like much of Samuel and Kings, in Deuteronomic style. This gives some account of Jeremiah's exploits, including a number of prose sermons attributed, like those of Samuel, Nathan, and others, to the prophet. The narrative purports to span the years 627 BC (1: 2) to 560 BC (52: 31), but, like the author of Kings, the author of the book of Jeremiah did not write with a purely historical aim. The ending is almost identical with that of 2 Kings, for example, and presumably has the same theological function (see pp. 80–1).

It is more than probable that the first of the two dates given in 1: 1–3 (namely 627 BC) is not historical, but intended to imply

that Jeremiah was active in Jerusalem in the years leading up to
Josiah's reformation in 622 BC (2 Kgs. 22–3; cf. 2 Chr. 34–5).
The same motive seems to have been responsible for placing
Ezra the religious leader before Nehemiah the architect in the
Chronicler's account of events in fifth-century BC Jerusalem. It is
certainly odd that Jeremiah is totally silent on the subject of
Josiah's reformation, and that all of Jeremiah's dated prophecies,
except 3: 6 ff. ('in the days of King Josiah'—the exception that
proves the rule?), come from the period covered by the second
date, that is to say from after the death of Josiah in 609 BC to the
fall of Jerusalem in 586 BC.

The prose passages include both biographical narrative such as
the story of the potter's flask (19), Jeremiah's letter to the exiles
(29), his suffering and imprisonment at the hands of the Jewish
hierarchy (36–45, which are sometimes attributed to Baruch his
amanuensis), and the prose sermons such as the Temple Sermon
(7; cf. 26: 1–24), and the New Covenant promises (31: 31–4),
often attributed to the Deuteronomist. A third source, containing
poetic passages known as the 'Confessions' (e.g. 18: 19–23; 20:
7–18), is often isolated and thought to be by the prophet himself.
This separation into three sources, however, one by Jeremiah, one
by Baruch, and one by the Deuteronomist, is not without its
problems. In any case the actual words of Baruch and Jeremiah
are certainly beyond our reach, and poetic beauty cannot seriously
be accepted as a very objective criterion for authenticity. The
prose sections surely contain some reminiscences of what Jeremiah
actually said and did, while the Confessions bear so striking a
resemblance to some of the psalms (e.g. 22, 44, 89) that one
cannot rule out the possibility that a Psalm may actually have been
placed on the lips of Jeremiah as in the case of Jonah (2) and
Habakkuk (3).

Doom-laden prophecies and sermons make up most of the
book, as one might expect from a man living in the shadow of
defeat and exile. All the more striking therefore are the rich
prophecies of hope that appear from time to time throughout the
book, e.g. 'Behold, the days are coming, says the Lord, when the
city shall be rebuilt for the Lord from the tower of Hananel to
the Corner Gate' (31: 38; cf. 33: 15).

Like the ending of Amos these are no doubt the products of that leap of faith so characteristic of the Exilic period and built into the fabric of biblical prophecy. Although not spoken by the original prophet himself, they are an integral part of the Jeremiah tradition, the Jeremiah who, when he saw smoke rising above Jerusalem in 586 BC, is reputed to have thought that it meant that his people were again bringing sacrifices to the Temple, and rejoiced. He is more often remembered for his gloomy complaints and forebodings, however, as the tradition that he wrote the book of Lamentations, desolate at the fate of his people and their city, illustrates: 'I am the man who has seen affliction under the rod of his wrath' (Lam. 3: 1).

Lamentations 5 is actually known as the 'Prayer of Jeremiah'. The apocryphal work attributed to Jeremiah is the letter of Jeremiah (= Baruch 6), addressed, like chapter 29, to Diaspora Jews and consisting of colourful attacks on idolatry reminiscent of parts of Isaiah 44–6 and Daniel.

In Jeremiah we find a closer intimacy between man and God than in other prophetic traditions. There are glimpses of this in the stories of Moses (Exod. 33; Deut. 34: 10), Elijah (1 Kgs. 19), and Isaiah (21: 1–4), but nowhere is it so richly and skilfully portrayed as in Jeremiah's Confessions, thus:

> Heal me, O Lord, and I shall be healed;
>> save me, and I shall be saved;
>> for thou art my praise.
> Behold, they say to me,
>> 'Where is the word of the Lord?
>> Let it come!'
> I have not pressed thee to send evil
>> nor have I desired the day of disaster,
>> thou knowest;
> that which came out of my lips
>> was before thy face.
> Be not a terror to me;
>> thou art my refuge in the day of evil.
> Let those be put to shame who persecute me,
>> but let me not be put to shame;

> let them be dismayed,
>> but let me not be dismayed;
> bring upon them the day of evil;
>> destroy them with double destruction! (17: 14–18)

He more than any can claim to have been 'in the council of the Lord' (23: 18–19). His sensitivity to Israel's wickedness and his consciousness that disaster was inevitable are such that most of the book is characterized by poignant lamentation, e.g.:

> My grief is beyond healing,
>> my heart is sick within me.
> Hark, the cry of the daughter of my people
>> from the length and breadth of the land:
> 'Is the Lord not in Zion.
>> Is her King not in her?'
> 'Why have they provoked me to anger with their graven images,
>> and with their foreign idols?'
> 'The harvest is past, the summer is ended,
>> and we are not saved.'
> For the wound of the daughter of my people is my heart wounded,
>> I mourn, and dismay has taken hold on me.
> Is there no balm in Gilead?
>> Is there no physician there?
> Why then has the health of the daughter of my people
>> not been restored?
> O that my head were waters,
>> and my eyes a fountain of tears,
> that I might weep day and night
>> for the slain of the daughter of my people!
>>>> (8: 18–9: 1.)

His intimacy manifests itself ultimately in his conviction that, despite Israel's horrifying disobedience and waywardness, God loves his people Israel with an everlasting love:

Behold the days are coming, says the Lord, when I will make a new covenant with the house of Israel and the house of Judah, not like the covenant which I made with their fathers when I took them by the hand to bring them out of the land of Egypt, my covenant which they broke, though I was their husband, says the Lord. But this is the covenant which I will make with the house of Israel after those days, says the Lord: I will put my law within them, and I will write it upon their hearts; and I will be their God and they shall be my people. And no longer shall each man teach his neighbour and each his brother, saying, 'Know the Lord,' for they shall all know me, from the least of them to the greatest, says the Lord, for I will forgive their iniquity, and I will remember their sin no more . . .

Thus says the Lord:
'If the heavens above can be measured,
    and the foundations of the earth below can be explored,
then I will cast off all the descendants of Israel
    for all that they have done.'

(31: 31–4, 37)

The Temple Sermon

Jeremiah 7 contains the words of a long and bitter sermon delivered by the prophet at the gate of the Temple of Jerusalem. It begins with an appeal to the people of Judah to mend their ways. If they stop oppressing the needy and worshipping other gods, he says, they will be able to live on the land that was given of old to their fathers (vv. 3–7). But apart from those short introductory words, the sermon holds out no flicker of hope for his people (7: 8–8: 3). Their crimes are ruthlessly catalogued. First, of all, in the words of the Ten Commandments (Exod. 20: 2–17), they steal, murder, commit adultery, swear falsely, and go after other gods (v. 9). They participate in the family worship of the Queen of Heaven (v. 18), a rite referred to again in chapter 44. They have rejected the prophets' call for obedience rather than ritual (vv. 21–6). They have taken part in all manner of ritual abominations, including child sacrifice (v. 31; cf. Ezek. 20: 25) and star worship (8: 2).

But that is not all. Contaminated by these and other hideous crimes, they have the gall to enter the Temple of the Lord expecting to be purified. They imagine that there is something

automatic about the holiness of God: by reciting some formula—
'This is the temple of the Lord, the temple of the Lord, the
temple of the Lord' (v. 4)—they can guarantee their immunity
from justice. It is this that the prophet challenges. If they treat
the Temple as a hideout for criminals escaping from justice, then
its holiness is removed: it becomes a 'den of robbers' (v. 11),
fit only for destruction. Far from their being sanctified by the
Temple, the Temple is desecrated by them. So the people will be
exiled (7: 14; 8: 3) or slaughtered (7: 32–3; 8: 1–2), the land
laid waste (7: 34), and the few survivors will wish they were
dead (8: 3).

This story of a prophet's attack on the Temple recurs with
variations in chapter 26 and in the Gospels (Matt. 21: 12–13;
Mark 11: 15–19; Luke 19: 45–7; John 2: 13–22). The Jeremiah
parallel contains the Shiloh image (26: 6; cf. 7: 12–14), the
Gospels the 'den of robbers'. Without allowing ourselves to be
sidetracked by the question of what actually happened and to what
extent one story has been influenced by another, we may safely
assume that Jeremiah and Jesus did attack the Temple in some
memorable incident or incidents, and that the six biblical accounts,
two in Jeremiah and four in the Gospels, are interpretations of such
events, each told in its own way. A comparison of the two Jeremiah
accounts reveals some interesting religious and theological insights
into how a prophet's words and actions were understood.

In the first place Jeremiah 7 tells us almost nothing about the
circumstances surrounding the delivery of the 'Temple Sermon',
apart from the reference in verse 2 to where it was delivered. No
date is given, and no account of the audience's reaction or of
what happened afterwards. Instead the words of the sermon are
presented at great length in six carefully constructed paragraphs.
Each unit is in the form of a prophecy of judgement, first describing the present situation, then foretelling future judgement with
the formula 'Therefore thus says the Lord ...' or 'therefore the
days are coming ...' (see pp. 30–2).

In chapter 26 the situation is exactly the reverse. The date
is given as the 'beginning of the reign of Jehoiakim', that is to
say 609 BC, and may imply that this was Jeremiah's first public
appearance (see p. 96). Only five verses are devoted to what

Jeremiah said (vv. 2–6). The rest of the chapter contains a blow-by-blow account of the effect of his sermon. The city was split between the religious establishment (priests and prophets) and the princes of Judah. At first Jeremiah was almost lynched by the people, incited apparently by the priests and prophets (vv. 7–9), but, thanks to the intervention of the princes, he was eventually given a fair hearing (vv. 12–15). 'Certain of the elders of the land' spoke up in his defence, adducing the parallel case of Micah who predicted the downfall of Jerusalem and was not put to death (vv. 17–19), and Jeremiah was saved. But the extent of the danger to his life at that time is highlighted by a chilling reference to what happened to another prophet who was executed by Jehoiakim (vv. 20–3) in similar circumstances. The two accounts nicely supplement each other, chapter 26 giving a colourful and convincing context for the isolated sermon in chapter 7.

A closer look at the two sermons, however, reveals substantial differences, not just in length. Both use the example of Shiloh, but in a different way. Shiloh was a familiar gaunt ruin by the roadside not far north of Jerusalem, and in chapter 26 the prophet uses it as a warning: 'If you will not listen to me . . . then I will make this house like Shiloh' (vv. 5–6). The people's reaction confirms this. He did not say Jerusalem would be destroyed; he called for repentance which would prevent its destruction. In chapter 7, however, the ruins of Shiloh are quoted as an illustration of what Jerusalem will inevitably become. It is too late for repentance. Jeremiah is explicitly instructed not to pray for his people (v. 16), as Isaiah (6: 11) and Amos (7: 2, 5) did.

These differences suggest that chapter 26 contains some account of what happened although little of what Jeremiah said, while chapter 7 is an elaborate rewriting of the sermon in the light of the actual destruction of the Temple and the Babylonian Exile. It is written, like so much of the book of Jeremiah and Joshua–Kings, in unmistakably Deuteronomic prose style. It addresses the question of why Jerusalem was destroyed, and seeks to explain it by reference to the enormity of the crimes perpetrated there. It focuses on the Temple as the heart of the problem, and perhaps paves the way for a more internalized, more spiritual religion, expressed, for example, in the notion of circumcision of the heart

(Deut. 30: 6), the sacrifice of a broken spirit (Ps. 51: 17), a Temple not built with hands (Isa. 66: 1–4; 2 Cor. 5: 1), and a new Jerusalem without a Temple (Rev. 21: 22). This brings us full circle to the possibility of salvation through repentance and a new heart after all (Jer. 7: 2–7; 26: 2–6; 31: 31–4).

Jeremiah 20: 7–18

In the last of the poems known as the Confessions of Jeremiah (p. 96), the intimacy and drama of the prophet's relationship with God reaches a climax. It is in two parts, separated by a short hymn of praise (v. 13).

The first part is a lament reminiscent of Psalm 22:

> O Lord, thou has deceived me,
> and I was deceived.

The lament may not of course contain the original words of the prophet, but it brilliantly describes the agony of a man facing doubt and persecution and fits perfectly into the story of Jeremiah as we have it. The repetition of the verb, first in the active and then in the passive voice, echoes 17: 14:

> Heal me, O Lord, and I shall be healed;
> save me, and I shall be saved.

The term translated 'deceive' (NEB 'seduce') is interesting. It occurs most often in contexts where an intimate, often clandestine, relationship is involved, between lovers, for example (Exod. 22: 11–12), and between Eve and the serpent (Gen. 3: 13). In a passage with obvious similarities to the present context (1 Kgs. 22: 20–2) a lying spirit is sent by God, through the mediation of a prophet, to *lure* King Ahab to his death. This seems to be the cry of a prophet suddenly doubting the truth of what he has been preaching. What if the prophecy immediately preceding this lament (in the present arrangement of the text), for example, should turn out to be false? What if the people of Judah are not taken captive to Babylon, and Pashhur the priest is not killed?

Verse 8 contains a two-word summary of this grim prophecy: 'Violence and destruction!'

For the reader there is dramatic irony in this because we know that the prophecy will shortly be fulfilled. But Jeremiah did not know for sure, and his contemporaries laughed at him, watching and waiting for him to be exposed as a false prophet. At times he could not bear this pressure and verses 7 and 8 give us a glimpse into this personal crisis of faith.

A second complaint concerns the inner compulsion that prophets experience. Balaam is the most spectacular biblical example: hired by the king of Moab to say one thing, compelled by God to say another (Num. 23: 4). But it is common to all prophets from Moses to Jonah (see pp. 5–6). Jeremiah felt it at the very beginning (Jer. 1: 4–10), and refers to it again here:

> If I say, 'I will not mention him,
>   or speak any more in his name,'
> there is in my heart as it were a burning fire
>   shut up in my bones,
> and I am weary with holding it in,
>   and I cannot.   (v. 9)

For a moment the prophet clutches at the remnants of his faith, reciting formulas about God's treatment of the righteous and the fate of those who persecute them (vv. 11–12), and part of a hymn of praise celebrating the power of God to 'deliver the life of the needy from the hand of evildoers' (v. 13). But then he sinks back into black despair, and, like Elijah (1 Kgs. 19: 4) and Jonah (4: 3, 8), wishes he was dead (vv. 14–18).

The second part of the poem is so closely parallel in form and thought to Job's lament (Job 3) that we must suppose a common source or dependence of one on the other. Ideas and images are developed almost to the point of burlesque. Job curses not just the day he was born but the night he was conceived (v. 3). The concentration of words for darkness in verses 4–6 is quite extraordinary. He imagines the day expunged from the calendar and God looking for it in vain (v. 4). He summons the professionals to assist him in his incantations against the day he was born (v. 8).

Jeremiah prays that the man responsible for announcing his birth and not killing him there and then be cursed like Sodom and Gomorrah (20: 15–16). Job beautifully develops the notion of death being a happier form of existence than life (3: 13–19). Jeremiah stops short at the grotesque thought that his mother would have been his grave 'and her womb for ever great' (20: 17).

Common to both poems is the bitterly nostalgic contrast between the joy that accompanied their birth and the misery that has befallen them since they grew up, as is the painful questioning that takes us back to the despair of Psalm 22:

> Why did I come forth from the womb to see toil and sorrow,
>   and spend my days in shame?'
>
> (Jer. 20: 18)

Ezekiel

So powerful is the chariot vision with which the book of Ezekiel opens that Jewish law restricted the reading or expounding of it:

The forbidden degrees [Lev. 18: 6–18] may not be expounded before three persons, nor the Story of Creation [Gen. 1: 1–3] before two, nor the Chariot [Ezek. 1] before one alone, unless he is a sage that understands of his own knowledge. Whosoever gives his mind to four things, it were better for him if he had not come into the world: What is above? What is beneath? What was before time? What will be hereafter? And whosoever takes no thought for the honour of his Maker it were better for him if he had not come into the world.' (Meg. 2: 1; Danby, pp. 212–13)

In fact the passage had a profound influence upon Judaism. It sparked off a whole line of mystical tradition known as Merkabah ('chariot') mysticism. Already within the Hebrew Bible there are signs of this (e.g. 1 Chr. 28: 18; Hab. 3: 8–9), and by the time the apocryphal book of Ecclesiasticus was written (*c.*180 BC), the chariot vision was the main part of the Ezekiel tradition to be alluded to: 'It was Ezekiel who saw the vision of glory which God showed him above the chariot of the cherubim' (Ecclus. 49: 8).

Very little is recorded of the life of this influential visionary. He was a priest (1: 3), he was married (24: 16–18), and his house was used from time to time as a meeting-place for the leaders of his community in Babylon (8: 1; 14: 1)—perhaps a kind of embryonic synagogue. His ministry spans the years 593 (1: 2) to 571 (29: 17).

After the call (1–3), his prophecies are preserved in four collections. The first apparently antedates the destruction of Jerusalem since it is addressed to the people of Judah and Jerusalem (4–24). Then comes a series of prophecies against the foreign nations (25–32). Chapters 33–9 offer hope to the survivors of the Babylonian invasion of 587–586; and finally there is the extraordinary vision of an ideal Temple, protected from impurity by massive fortifications, and of a miraculous river which rises from under its threshold and brings new life and health into the Promised Land (40–8).

It may be that the first part of the book goes back to a period in the prophet's life when he was active in Jerusalem, although there is no trace of this in the book as we have it now. Of all the prophets he is represented as the most otherworldly, not only in terms of his preoccupation with Temple rituals and condemnations of ritual impurities, but also in the spectacular visions and trances he experiences. In addition to the vision of the chariot, with its gleaming wheels and fabulous beasts (1), and the Temple vision (40–8), there is the eerie visit to the Temple, lifted by a lock of hair between earth and heaven and brought by the spirit to Jerusalem (8–11), the resurrection of the dead in the valley of dry bones (37), and the eschatological defeat of Gog and Magog (38–9).

Moreover, no other prophet clothes his message in such elaborate figures and images. On the one hand, there are the extended allegories of the shipwreck of Tyre (27), the punishment of Pharaoh, the 'great crocodile wallowing in the Nile' (29: 3–7 JB), and the 'Descent into the Underworld' (32; cf. Isaiah 14). On the other, there are the extraordinary parables which he is described as acting out in his daily life; e.g. knocking a hole in the wall of his house and crawling through it in the middle of the night with his luggage (12: 1–7; cf. 4: 1–5: 6; see pp. 11–13). It is easy to see how it came about that Ezekiel was a source for later apocalyptists, such as the author of Revelation, who quotes Ezekiel or alludes to him more than to any other part of scripture, and the author of the Temple Scroll from Qumran.

At the heart of this visionary book there are profound spiritual and theological truths which break new ground in the history of biblical thought and raise Ezekiel to the ranks of the great theologians of later times. In the first place, he puts a new emphasis on individual responsibility, e.g.:

The soul that sins shall die. The son shall not suffer for the iniquity of the father, nor the father suffer for the iniquity of the son; the righteousness of the righteous shall be upon himself, and the wickedness of the wicked shall be upon himself. But if a wicked man turns away from all his sins which he has committed and keeps all my statutes and does what is lawful and right, he shall surely live; he shall not die. (18: 20–1)

This leads him to the revolutionary idea that his people cannot rely on their past history: 'Thus says the Lord God to Jerusalem: Your origin and your birth are of the land of the Canaanites; your father was an Amorite, and your mother a Hittite' (16: 3).

There is very little in Ezekiel about the promise to Abraham (33: 24 is a revealing exception) or the Sinai covenant. But, like Paul, he speaks of forgiveness in an everlasting covenant, e.g.:

I will make a covenant of peace with them; it shall be an everlasting covenant with them; and I will bless them and multiply them, and will set my sanctuary in the midst of them for evermore. My dwelling place shall be with them, and I will be their God, and they shall be my people. (37: 26–7; cf. Jer. 31: 1; 2 Cor. 6: 16; Rev. 21: 3)

Although not expressed in the same affectionate language, the idea comes close to Hosea 1–3, Deuteronomy 6, and Isa. 49: 15. Ezekiel is throughout concerned with the inner experience of the individual, in particular a 'new heart and a new spirit': e.g. 'A new heart I will give you, and a new spirit I will put within you; and I will take out of your flesh the heart of stone and give you a heart of flesh' (36: 26; cf. 11: 19; 18: 31; see p. 56). Even the Messiah is less a triumphant king than a shepherd, caring for his sheep (34:

23), and the feasts of the Passover and Tabernacles are times to make atonement for sins (45: 18–25), rather than joyful celebrations as they are in the Pentateuch. If Ezekiel is to be called the 'Father of Judaism', then it is not a ritualistic or legalistic Judaism, but that rich spiritual strand of Judaism that manifested itself when the temple lay in ruins, first in the sixth century BC and later, after AD 70: as also in the new spirit advocated by Paul (e.g. 2 Cor. 3: 3) and in the visions of a new world and a new Jerusalem in the book of Revelation (21–2).

Ezekiel 11

Chapter 11 rounds off the visionary experience that befell Ezekiel in September 592 BC, by describing the departure of 'the glory of the God of Israel' from Jerusalem (v. 23) and the return of the prophet, carried by the spirit, to Babylon, where he recounts his vision to the exiles (vv. 24–5). With considerable literary skill, which does not always go hand in hand with historical interest, the author of chapters 8–11 gathers up several earlier themes. Chapter 11 is in three parts: prophecies of judgement (vv. 1–13), a prophecy of hope (vv. 14–21), and the concluding narrative (vv. 22–5).

The scene is set at the east gate of the Temple (v. 1), that is to say the gate which looks across the Valley of the Kedron towards the Mount of Olives. The 'divine chariot' is already there (10: 19), and the prophet, transported there by the spirit 'by a lock of his head' (8: 3), joins it. He is commanded to prophesy to twenty-five men, presumably the same men who were caught in the act of participating in some obscene religious rite earlier in the narrative (8: 16–17). Here they are accused of bad government (v. 2) and the slaughter of innocent people (v. 6). This lurid charge is levelled against Manesseh by the author of 2 Kings (e.g. 21: 16), but here could refer to such a case as that of the murder of Uriah the prophet in the days of Jehoiakim (Jer. 26: 20–23).

The cauldron image (vv. 3, 7, 11), perhaps less quaint-sounding to the prophet's original audience than to us today, is double-edged. It stands, on the one hand, for toughness and impenetrability (vv. 3–4). On the other, it is a vessel that boils and kills its contents over the intense heat of a log fire (v. 7; cf. 24: 3–4). Jerusalem is the cauldron, where God's people are safe (e.g. Ps. 48); but not for ever. When the king of Babylon lays siege to it, it will become an inferno. The 'contents' are, first, the twenty-five who see themselves as in a position of invincible power in Jerusalem (v. 3) and refuse to accept that their days are numbered. With characteristic irony the prophet turns this cauldron image round, to accuse them of filling it, that is Jerusalem, with the mangled flesh of their innocent victims (v. 7).

Apart from these few striking details the prophecy is written in stereotyped prose, punctuated with the formula '... and you shall know that I am the Lord' (vv. 10, 12).

The two prophecies are separated by a remarkable verse, telling of the sudden death of one of the twenty-five, Pelatiah the son of Benaiah, and the agony of the prophet apparently appalled at the devastating effect of his preaching. Like Moses, Jeremiah, and Amos, Ezekiel intercedes for his people: 'Ah Lord God! Wilt thou make a full end of the remnant of Israel?' (v. 13).

The second part of the chapter is a prophecy of salvation addressed to the exiles in Babylon (vv. 14–21). It contains several powerful expressions of hope. First, the remarkable statement 'I have been a sanctuary to them for a while' (RSV) or perhaps better 'a small sanctuary for them in the countries where they have gone' (v. 16). The word for 'sanctuary' is the same as that used in 8: 6; 9: 6; 44: 1, 5, 7, 8, 9, and elsewhere of the Temple at Jerusalem. The notion that, even after the Temple was destroyed, God's presence was with his people picks up a theme from the wilderness tradition (e.g. Exod. 25: 8), reinforced perhaps by the first appearance of a synagogue of some kind among the exiles. It may be that the prophet's house at some stage functioned as a religious meeting-place (cf. 8: 1; 14: 1).

Secondly, although the general sense of the expressions 'one heart' and 'new spirit' is clear (cf. Jer. 31: 31; Ps. 51: 10), the specific terms used here are unusual. Elsewhere Ezekiel has 'new heart' (18: 31; 36: 26), but as it stands the text wishes to convey the sense of single-mindedness, as in Jer. 32: 39, especially in a context where people are depicted as assembling from all over the world. The two phrases together suggest singleness of purpose as well as a new beginning. Elsewhere Ezekiel stresses individual responsibility (e.g. 14: 12–20; 18); but that is no reason to assume that he did not also believe in the merits of single-mindedness. The sequel confirms this: 'they shall be my people, and I will be their God' (v. 20). Verse 21 keeps open the possibility, however, that unregenerate individuals, who continue to defy God, will be punished.

The chapter ends with a final glimpse of the 'chariot', with whose awesome appearance in a 'great cloud, with brightness round about it, and fire flashing forth continually' (1: 4) the book of Ezekiel began. As it moved away from Jerusalem, 'the cherubim lifted up their wings with the wheels beside them; and the glory of the God of Israel was over them' (v. 22). The cherubim were living creatures, each with four wings, two to cover their bodies and two stretched out straight, one toward another, like the cherubim over the ark (Exod. 25: 20). So far the description is that of a throne (1: 26). But the wheels give it also the appearance of a chariot (cf. Hab. 3: 8; Isa. 66: 15). When the throne-chariot moved, the wings of the cherubim made a sound like the sound of many waters, like the thunder of the Almighty, a sound of tumult like the sound of a host (1: 23–4).

It moved (43: 1–3) east and stood over the Mount of Olives, temporarily exiled from Jerusalem, like King David during the revolt of Absalom his son (2 Sam. 15), and there awaited the building of a new city to be called 'The Lord is there' (Ezek. 48: 35). The picture is one of hovering nearby, not travelling to the exiles in Babylon. Ezekiel, however, did return to tell them all the things that the Lord had shown him, including the notion of a 'small sanctuary' which would ensure the Lord's presence with them in exile, until the time came for them to return to their homeland (vv. 16–17).

Ezekiel 37: 1–14

It might be helpful to call this most familiar of all Ezekiel's visions the '*ruah* vision' instead of the 'Vision of the dry bones', because, although it may not appear so in the English versions, the word *ruah* occurs ten times in the fourteen verses of the passage. In the

RSV it is translated 'spirit' at the beginning and end of the passage (vv. 1 and 14), 'wind' in verse 9, and elsewhere 'breath'. Of course *ruaḥ* does not mean 'spirit of God', 'wind', and 'breath of life' all at once. But no author could have written these verses without being aware of the connections.

This leads us to another preliminary observation. The only two passages in which the term 'Spirit of the Lord' occurs are this one and chapter 11, and it can hardly be a coincidence that these are two of the three passages where the prophet envisages a time when the Lord God puts a new *ruaḥ* in his people. The other passage where this idea is expressed is chapter 36: 'And a new *ruaḥ* I will put within you . . . I will put my *ruaḥ* within you' (v. 27), corresponding closely to 37: 14, the climax of the 'Vision of the dry bones'. Surely we are expected to pick up this connection between 11, 36, and 37. At all events we clearly must approach chapter 37 as a vision about *ruaḥ*, in all its meanings, and in particular about the return of *ruaḥ* to the corpses abandoned by the glory of God in chapter 11.

The passage is autobiographical like most of Ezekiel, but unusual in its structure. It begins with an account of the vision, complete in itself (v. 1–10), but then adds an interpretation based on the saying: 'Our bones are dried up, and our hope is lost; we are clean cut off' (v. 11). Probably the vision itself was inspired by this saying, and the prophecies about 'a new *ruaḥ*' in chapters 11 and 36 just discussed. But whether it entailed an actual visionary experience or not, we cannot say.

The English versions fail to do justice to the opening formula 'the hand of the Lord was upon me'. 'The hand of the Lord was laid upon me *or* came upon me' would be better. The Hebrew for 'was' is frequently translated 'came to pass' or the like, when it describes an event not a state of affairs. Here it expresses the prophet's sudden experience of being possessed by God (see p. 8).

'The Spirit of the Lord' points back to chapter 11, as we saw; perhaps also Genesis 2 where the Lord God breathed life into the nostrils of the first man (Gen. 2: 7). 'The valley' or 'plain' takes us back to Ezekiel 3, scene of the prophet's earlier visions. It was there that the prophet himself felt the new power of God's *ruaḥ*, which he describes in identical terms: 'But the spirit entered into me and set me on my feet' (3: 24; cf. 37: 10). The bones are described as 'very dry', which implies they have been dead a long time, and 'very many', an indication of the enormity of the disaster. Verse 11 spells it out.

The rapid fulfilment of prophecy is a theme we met in chapter 11. No sooner does the prophet speak than the bones start to move together to form human skeletons again, and to be covered with sinews, flesh, and skin. The mention of the uncanny noise caused by the miracle recalls the mysterious noise Ezekiel had heard from the 'chariot' in chapter 1.

The final stage in the process of reviving Israel is approached as a separate creative act. In verses 5–6 it is mentioned twice; and in verses 9–10 it is the subject of a separate prophecy. It is explicitly referred to again in verse 14, and every time it is mentioned it is followed by the words 'and you/they shall live' (vv. 5, 6, 9, 14), or 'and they lived, and stood upon their feet, an exceedingly great host' (v. 10). Again perhaps 'live' in Hebrew is more dynamic, and should be translated 'came to life', an event rather than a state. Notice again how close the language of this verse is to that describing the prophet's own experience in 3: 24. One cannot separate the two narratives, even if in translation one may prefer 'breath' in one and 'spirit' in the other.

One detail, however, differs from the parallels in Genesis 2 and Ezekiel 3, 11, and 36: 'Come from the four winds, O *ruaḥ* (v. 9). It is certainly a mysterious wind that blows in four directions at once (if that is the meaning), although, if it is God's spirit, which 'blows where it wills' (John 3: 8), it would be understandable. Alternatively, could there be an allusion to the four spirits (or winds) in the wheels of the 'chariot' (1: 15–21)?

Verses 12–13 introduce a new theme, not entirely consistent with what has gone before. Up till now we have had a picture of something like a battlefield strewn with unburied corpses. The mention of graves in this verse does not fit such a description. We might suppose that it is the answer to an unspoken question such as the following: 'But what about those who are lost to view, buried in distant lands? Is there hope for them too?' The answer is that this vision concerns 'the whole house of Israel' (v: 11). The resurrection of the dead in verse 12 is a statement to that effect (like Isa. 26: 19), and the last words of the passage identify that 'resurrection' with return to the promised land (v. 14; cf. 11: 17; 36: 28).

6

The Prophets (III): Daniel to Malachi

Daniel

IN the Christian canon, Daniel is promoted from the Writings to a place among the Major Prophets, alongside Isaiah, Jeremiah, and Ezekiel. He is not actually called a prophet in the book and, although his visions, his trances, his ability to predict, his intercession for his people (9), and his challenging of royal authorities roughly fit the conventional prophetic role, the language, style, imagery and content of the book are in most respects very different from any other prophet. In fact Daniel (alongside Noah and Job) is remembered as one of three men who 'delivered their own lives by their righteousness' (Ezek. 14: 14), and this is actually how he is represented in the book that bears his name.

He is introduced in chapter 1 as one of a number of 'youths without blemish, handsome and skilful in all wisdom, endowed with knowledge, understanding and learning . . .' (1: 4) at the court of the king of Babylon. He and his three friends stand firm against all kinds of threat: risking their lives to observe the food laws, for example (1: 8–16), choosing death in the 'burning fiery furnace' rather than idolatry (chap. 3), or facing the lions' den rather than renounce their faith (chap. 6).

Much of the book is taken up with visions and their interpretations, but the conclusion returns once more to the theme of righteousness: 'And those who are wise shall shine like the brightness of the firmament; and those who turn many to righteousness, like the stars for ever and ever' (12: 3).

Of the various apocryphal additions to Daniel (written in Greek probably in the second or first century BC, and therefore not included in the Hebrew Bible), three continue the tale of Daniel's righteousness: how he rescued Susanna from the wicked elders ('a Daniel come to judgement'), exposed the impotence of Babylon's two idols, Bel and the Dragon, and converted the king to Judaism (Dan. 14: 28, 41).

Clearly the book of Daniel is a collection of legends and visions from a variety of sources clustered around a popular folk-hero. His visions, which are firmly dated to the reigns of Nebuchadnezzar, Belshazzar, Cyrus, and Darius, describe the downfall of earthly kingdoms, the coming of one like a son of man with clouds of glory (7: 13), the rebuilding of Jerusalem, the persecution of God's people, and the resurrection of the dead 'at the time of the end' (12). For those who believed that these visions were being fulfilled in their own day, like the early Christians (cf. Matt. 24: 30; 26: 64; Mark 13: 26; 14: 62; Luke 21: 27; 22: 69; Rev. 14: 14), then Daniel was first and foremost a prophet, contemporary of Jeremiah, Ezekiel, Haggai, and Zechariah.

There is every reason to suppose that the book was in fact written in the second century BC, during the Maccabean crisis. A large section is written, like part of Ezra, in Aramaic (2: 4b–7: 28), which suggests a date not earlier than 400 BC, and some Greek words, notably among the musical instruments in 3: 5–6, point to a still later date. The developed angelology (Gabriel and Michael are both named: 8: 16; 10: 13, 12: 1), the symbolism of numbers (e.g. 7: 25; 12: 11–12), strange beasts (e.g. chap. 8), metals (chap. 2), and other terms suggest comparison with Joel and Zechariah 9–14 (see pp. 122–3), completed towards the end of the fourth century BC. The developed eschatology of chapter 12 points to a still later date, as do the minute details of the last vision (chap. 11). This describes the reign of Antiochus IV Epiphanes (175–163 BC) so accurately and so poignantly that we may conclude that the author himself lived through it, e.g. 'Forces from him shall appear and profane the temple and fortress, and shall take away the continual burnt offering. And they shall set up the abomination that makes desolate. He shall seduce with flattery those who violate the covenant; but the people who know their God shall stand firm and take action.' (11: 31–2; cf. 1 Macc. 1: 54).

The end of this final vision, however, transcends history since it represents the author's view of the future. He believed that the crisis was almost over and the end of the present age very near (12: 1–4). Whether prophecy or apocalyptic or, like Joel, Zechariah 9–14, and Isaiah 24–7, on the borderline between the two, the book of Daniel gives us a thrilling insight into beliefs and speculations current among the Jews at a crucial watershed in their history. New questions were raised about the nature of God, the course of world history, the fate of martyrs, and what happens after death. Daniel's fantastic visions are early attempts to tackle such questions, and from them Judaism and Christianity inherited the concept of history as a decline from a golden age to 'iron mixed with miry clay' (2: 36–45), the image of God as 'the Ancient of Days' (7: 9 ff.), the belief that the suffering of the martyrs refines and cleanses them to make them white until the time of the end (11: 34), and the doctrine of the resurrection of the dead, 'some to everlasting life and some to shame and everlasting contempt'. (12: 3).

Daniel 7

In addition to the earliest explicit reference in the Bible to the resurrection of the dead, Daniel also contains a unique 'son of man' passage. The elaborate vision in chapter 7 (at the end of the Aramaic section, 2: 4b–7: 28) begins with the appearance out of the great sea of four grotesque beasts—a lion with eagle's wings, a bear with three ribs in its jaws, a four-headed leopard with four wings, and 'a fourth beast, terrible and dreadful and exceedingly strong' with iron teeth and ten horns—and ends with the appearance of 'one like a son of man', that is of human appearance in contrast to the creatures that had gone before:

> And to him was given dominion
>   and glory and kingdom,
> that all peoples, nations, and languages
>   should serve him;
> his dominion is an everlasting dominion,
>   which shall not pass away,
> and his kingdom one
>   that shall not be destroyed   (7: 14)

Supervising the whole scene sits 'one that was ancient of days', enthroned on a fiery chariot reminiscent of Ezekiel 1 and surrounded by ten thousand times ten thousand.

Attention focuses on the fourth beast which 'was different from all the rest' (v. 19) and its little horn with eyes and a mouth which 'made war with the saints, and prevailed over them' (vv. 20–1). Not only is this last part of the vision repeated a second time in an expanded version, after the appearance of the Ancient of Days and the son of man (vv. 19–22), but it is interpreted in much greater detail than the earlier parts (vv. 23–7). Verse 25, for example, refers to the persecution of the Jews under Antiochus IV (175–164 BC):

> He shall be different from the former ones,
>   and shall put down three kings.
> He shall speak words against the Most High,
>   and shall wear out the saints of the Most High,
>   and shall think to change the times and the law;
> and they shall be given into his hand
>   for a time, two times, and half a time.   (vv. 24–5)

The first chapter of 1 Maccabees tells the story in greater detail, and 'a time, two times and half a time' seems to refer to the period of three and a half years from 167–164, when the 'abomination of desolation' was set up in the Temple (Dan. 8: 13; 11: 31; 1 Macc. 1: 54). The number three and a half, however, is also symbolic for a very short time, being half the whole number seven. The victory of the saints, mentioned both in the vision (vv. 21–2) and the interpretation (vv. 18, 25, 27), is not explained, however. In contrast to the detailed references to events leading up to and including the reign of Antiochus IV (cf. 8: 23–5; 11: 21–45), there is nothing in the book of Daniel to suggest that the author witnessed the victories of Judas Maccabaeus (1 Macc. 3 ff.) or knew that the crisis would last only three and a half years. His visions reflect years of persecution and his hopes for the future transcend the facts of history, e.g. 'by no human hand, he shall be broken' (8: 25; cf. 11: 45).

It is against this background that the son of man passage in 7:

13–14 must be viewed. Unlike the beasts that emerge from the great sea, he seems to come from heaven, and unlike the beasts no interpretation is given for him (v. 17). Unlike the saints of the Most High, he apparently has no role in the war (vv. 21–2). He is surely to be interpreted as a second heavenly being, alongside the Ancient of Days, and more like 'Michael, the great prince who is in charge of your people' (12: 1) than the symbolic beasts of this and the other vision in chapter 8. This view is supported by the famous vision of Enoch, which is clearly dependent on Daniel 7:

And there I saw one who had a head of days, and his head was white like wool; and with him there was another, whose face had the appearance of a man, and his face was full of grace, like one of the holy angels. And I asked one of the holy angels who went with me, and showed me all the secrets, about that Son of Man, who he was and whence he was and why he went with the Head of Days. And he answered me and said to me: 'This is the Son of Man who has righteousness and with whom righteousness dwells; he will reveal all the treasures of that which is secret, for the Lord of Spirits has chosen him... even before the sun and the constellations were created, before the stars of heaven were made, his name was named before the Lord of Spirits. He will be a staff to the righteous and holy and he will be the light of the nations, and he will be the hope of those who grieve in their hearts...' (Enoch 46: 1–3; 48: 3–4).

It is also the basis of several passages in which the 'son of man' language is applied to Jesus, e.g. 'And then they will see the Son of Man coming in clouds with great power and glory. And then he will send out the angels, and gather his elect from the four winds, from the ends of the earth to the ends of heaven' (Mark 13: 26–7; cf. Matt. 24: 30; Rev. 1: 7, 13). Of course the phrase often means no more than 'human being, one of human appearance', in contrast to beasts, but these are obvious allusions to the Daniel passage where it is rich in apocalyptic associations. We may further assume that our author, as yet unaware of how the crisis would end, had in mind, not earthly victories, but rather an eschatological kingdom, in which 'many of those that sleep in the dust of the earth shall awake, some to everlasting life, and some to shame and everlasting contempt' (Dan. 12: 2). Perhaps Paul's discussion of the resurrection of the dead contains a further variation on the heavenly 'son of man' theme: 'Just as we have borne the image of the man of dust, we shall also bear the image of the man of heaven. I tell you this, brethren: flesh and blood cannot inherit the kingdom of God, nor does the perishable inherit the imperishable. Lo! I tell you a mystery. We shall not all sleep . . .' (1 Cor. 15: 49–51).

The twelve Minor Prophets

Hosea

The book of Hosea is the longest of the twelve and in it, more than anywhere else, in spite of many textual and exegetical problems, we can hear the original voice of eighth-century prophecy speaking out boldly against materialism and social injustice. Here appear for the first time a spiritual dimension and an ethical idealism which were to have a profound influence on later tradition, including Paul and early Christianity. Maybe Hosea's was the first in the long sequence of radical voices of biblical prophecy.

Almost nothing is known of his life apart from oblique references in the book that bears his name. He was apparently a contemporary of Isaiah (1: 1; cf. Isa. 1: 1), witness therefore to the downfall of affluent Israel and the Assyrian invasions of 734–721 BC (cf. 5: 13; 7: 11; cf. Isa. 30: 1–5; 31: 1–3). His sufferings at the hands of an unreceptive people are alluded to in 9: 7–8, and if the first three chapters are based on his personal experience, as seems likely, we can add an unhappy marriage to his biography. A sad, often wistful character emerges from this beautiful book but one who is not afraid to challenge authority, including priests (4: 4–11) and kings (5: 1–7; 8: 4–7), with demands for justice and love, and one who can also predict a great future for Israel.

The book is a collection of prophecies, most of which can without much discussion be ascribed to the eighth century, and shows little sign of careful literary structure. It divides broadly into three sections. The first (chapters 1–3) concerns God's love for Israel, poignantly compared to Hosea's undying love for his disloyal wife (see p. 120). The backward look to the simple virtues of the wilderness period became a recurring theme in later tradition (cf. Deut. 32: 10–14; Jer. 7: 21–2), as did the naming of sons (cf. Isa. 7: 3, 14; 8: 3) and the image of God and Israel as man and wife (2: 16; 3: 1). In Christian tradition the image was applied to the mystical union between Christ and the Church, as it is also in the interpretation of the Song of Solomon.

The second section of the book (4: 1–9: 9) contains a long series of bitter prophecies of judgement, attacking idolatry, hypocrisy, and injustice in the land. Hosea's blend of firmness and compassion is unique in eighth-century prophecy, but typical of Deuteronomy and Jeremiah, e.g.:

> What shall I do with you, O Ephraim?
> What shall I do with you, O Judah?
> Your love is like a morning cloud,
>   like the dew that goes early away.

> Therefore I have hewn them by the prophets,
>   I have slain them by the words of my mouth,
>   and my judgment goes forth as the light.
> For I desire steadfast love and not sacrifice,
>   the knowledge of God, rather than burnt offerings.
>   (Hos. 6: 4–6)

The last section contains further attacks on Israel and Judah, but introduces a number of allusions, unique in early prophecy, to Israel's early traditions, including Baalpeor (9: 10; cf. Num. 25: 1–5), Jacob wrestling with the angel (12: 4; cf. Gen. 32: 24–8), and the prophet who brought Israel up from Egypt (12: 13; cf. Deut. 18: 15, 18; 34: 10–12). Through it all runs the theme of God's love:

> When Israel was a child, I loved him,
>   and out of Egypt I called my son . . .
> How can I give you up, O Ephraim!
> How can I hand you over, O Israel! . . .

> My heart recoils within me,
>   my compassion grows warm and tender.
>   (11: 1, 8; cf. 11: 3–4; 14: 4)

The vision with which the book ends gathers all these themes together, and need not be a later addition (like Amos 9: 11–15):

> I will heal their faithlessness;
>   I will love them freely,
>   for my anger has turned from them.
> I will be as the dew to Israel;
>   he shall blossom as the lily
>   he shall strike root as the poplar;
> his shoots shall spread out;
>   his beauty shall be like the olive,
>   and his fragrance like Lebanon.   (Hos. 14: 4–6)

Hosea 2: 14–23

This beautiful passage combines prophecies of renewal and restoration with the language of courtship and marriage, and is Hosea's most eloquent statement of faith in God's love for his wayward people. It is sharply separated from what precedes it in several ways. First there is the oracular formula 'says the Lord' (JB 'oracle of the Lord') which marks the end of the previous prophecy (vv. 2–13). It is significant that the name of God has not been mentioned since chapter 1, so that its reappearance here marks an abrupt change of direction in the prophet's words. In fact the prophecies of salvation which follow presuppose no change of heart, no repentance since the state of godlessness and immorality in verses 2–13. In Paul's terms, God showed his love to his people 'while we were yet sinners' (Rom. 5: 8; cf. Hos. 14: 4).

The passage has an impressive internal structure too. It is in two parts, each consisting of two prophecies: the first in each case is about a change of landscape, the second, introduced by the formula 'in that day, says the Lord', is about changes of name. At every stage verbal allusions back to the previous prophecy of judgement heighten the effect of these pictures of salvation.

In the first part (vv. 14–17), the wilderness that had previously threatened to kill Israel with thirst (v. 3) is transformed into the setting for tender love-making. Part of the wilderness, the Valley of Achor, is mentioned specifically by name. It had been the place where Achan was stoned and burned to death, and its sinister associations—even the name suggests 'bad luck, trouble' (e.g. Judg. 11: 35; 1 Kgs. 18: 17; Prov. 11: 29)—were commemorated with 'a great heap of stones that remains to this day' (Josh. 7: 22–6). The nostalgic hope that the old relationship between God and Israel, 'as in the days of her youth' (v. 15), would be renewed occurs in similar terms in Jer. 2: 2. But the tradition that the wilderness period was a golden age is not found elsewhere (cf. Ps. 95: 8–11; Jer. 7: 25; Exod. 17: 1–4; 32).

The change of name (v. 16) points back to verse 2: the one who denied he was her husband then, now accepts the title. Combined with the name-changing theme is the statement that the Baal-worship that led her so tragically astray (vv. 12–13) will be removed.

The second part starts with a prophecy that the land will be transformed and a new age will dawn for Israel. Beasts that threatened to devour her earlier (v. 12) will become her friends in a covenant relationship like the one imagined by Eliphaz in Job 5: 23, and weapons of war will be destroyed (v. 18). 'Grain, wine and oil', of which she had previously been deprived (vv. 5, 8, 9), will be restored to her (v. 22).

Verses 19–20 enrich the marriage terminology with six major theological terms, characterizing the new relationship between God and Israel, his bride. These are constituent parts of the relationship and at the same time its fruits (e.g. 4: 4; 6: 6; 10: 12; 12: 6): 'righteousness' (*zedek*: see p. 44); 'justice' (see p. 43); 'steadfast love' (or perhaps better 'generosity', to distinguish this word (*hesed*) from 'faithfulness'(*emunah*) in the next verse); 'love'; 'faithfulness' (or 'loyalty'); and 'the knowledge of God'. In the first five, God is the initiator; the sixth is about Israel's response: 'and you shall know the Lord'. 'Know' here goes beyond mere recognition, however. On the one hand it refers to the intimate relationship between kinsfolk (e.g. husband and wife) or close friends, and on the other to 'wisdom', that is to say all that can be learnt about God and how to love and obey him (e.g. 4: 4; 6: 6). Later tradition, for example, saw that 'knowledge of God' comes through study of the Torah.

Finally, the new relationship is sealed in the traditional way, by the changing of names. Jezreel, Hosea's first son, now means 'God sows' not 'God scatters' as in chapter 1; his daughter's name Lo-ruhamah 'Not-pitied' is changed to Ruhamah 'pitied'; and his other son Lo-ammi 'Not my people' is changed to Ammi 'my people'. These names are not merely symbols of the new situation. The changes are made before witnesses: heaven and earth are called in elsewhere for this purpose (e.g. Isa. 1: 2; Deut. 32: 1). In this way the restored relationship is made legally binding, and the concluding formula 'I shall be your God and you shall be my people' (cf. Jer. 31: 33; Ezek. 11: 20; 36: 28), here personalized in a very moving way, brings this prophecy of a renewed family of God to a close.

Joel

Like Hosea, Joel begins with a story, fact or fiction (we do not know), which dramatically epitomizes the prophet's theme. The invasion of locusts, a tale of brutal destruction, wailing, and lamentations, provides the language and imagery for the 'Day of the Lord' prophecies that make up most of the book. Joel's canonical position among the eighth-century prophets is due to the belief that his prophecies antedate the Assyrian invasions of Judah, since Assyria is conspicuous by its absence from the book, and indirectly predict them. The apocalyptic style and imagery of the book and a reference to the Greeks (3: 6) suggest a fourth-century date (contemporary of Zech. 9–14). Repeated references to the darkening of the sun (2: 10, 31; 3: 15; cf. 2: 2) may well reflect the unparalled phenomenon of three total eclipses of the sun visible in Jerusalem during that century (p. 89). In Christian tradition he is the prophet of Pentecost, quoted by Peter at some length in Acts 2: 14–21:

For these men are not drunk, as you suppose, since it is only the third hour of the day; but this is what was spoken of by the prophet Joel: 'And in the last days it shall be, God declares, that I will pour out my Spirit upon all flesh, and your sons and your daughters will prophesy, and your young men shall see visions, and your old men shall dream dreams; yea, and on my menservants and my maidservants in those days, I will pour out my spirit; and they shall prophesy...' (Acts 2: 15 ff.)

Two striking features of Joel set him apart from eighth-century prophecy. First, although empty ritualism is fleetingly condemned in the famous line: 'Rend your hearts and not your garments' (2: 13), this is the exception. Joel in all other respects frames his prophecies in cultic terms: e.g. 'Gird on sackcloth (1: 13)... sanctify a fast (1: 14)... blow the trumpet in Zion (2: 1, 15)... between the altar and the vestibule, let the priests, the ministers of the Lord weep...' (2: 17). No doubt he was a priest, but was he also addressing priests, calling for repentance within the religious establishment?

Secondly, he more than any other prophet draws on traditional language and imagery to express radical new ideas, e.g.

> Beat your ploughshares into swords,
>   and your pruning hooks into spears;
>   let the weak say, 'I am a warrior'.
>   (3. 10; cf. Isa. 2: 4; Mic. 4: 3)

Nowhere, is the Day of the Lord more colourfully described, both the life and vision of a new age, and the horrors of confrontation between the powers of good and evil 'in the valley of decision' (3: 14). Like Zechariah 9–14, Joel bridges the gap between prophecy and apocalyptic, but unlike Zechariah he remains firmly within the prophetic tradition.

Amos

In the Book of Amos we have the earliest collection of a prophet's original words. This may well be due to the fact that his predictions, unlike those of his predecessors, were fulfilled soon after he made them, and to the literary activity of 'the men of Hezekiah' (714–686 BC), who, according to Prov. 25: 1, 'copied' some of Solomon's proverbs. However that may be, the words of Amos probably go back to the first half of the eighth century BC, before the Assyrian invasions which began under Tiglath Pileser III in 734 BC. There is no explicit reference to Assyria in Amos, for example, or to the covenant, which one would expect in later compositions. Idolatry is another subject conspicuous by its absence from the words of Amos, and the overwhelming predominance of judgement, with barely a whisper of hope, likewise belongs to a period of relative peace, prosperity, and, at least on the part of Israel's powerful leaders to whom Amos's words were addressed, hypocritical religiosity and injustice. His task was to widen their horizons and open their eyes, on the one hand, to the plight of the poor in their land, and at the same time to the vulnerability of Israel in the world of eighth-century BC international politics. He was not the only prophet to live during the affluent reign of Jeroboam: Jonah ben Amittai was a contemporary (2 Kgs. 14: 25–7).

The last few verses of the book of Amos clearly date from a later age (see below) and have the effect of creating another Amos, a fictitious prophet who sees beyond the darkness of the present tragic century to a happier time in the future, when ' "I will restore the fortunes of my people Israel . . . and they shall never again be plucked up out of the land which I have given them", says the Lord your God' (9: 14–15). For those who heed this call for repentance (e.g. 5: 14), there will be hope beyond judgement.

The freshness and variety of Amos's style suggest a considerable degree of literary expertise, and the allusions to events and conditions in neighbouring lands confirm that he was no country bumpkin. Although disclaiming any formal association with 'the sons of the prophets' (i.e. the professional prophets: 7: 14), it is likely that he was well versed in traditional techniques. His use of legal idioms and forms, his exciting variations on the messenger speech form (see p. 30), and the effective inclusion of such fine poetic compositions (not necessarily from his own hand) as the creation hymns in chapters 4, 5, and 9 and the lament in chapter 5 (see pp. 34–5), make up an impressive list. Amos belongs firmly in the line of prophets that began in Israel before the eighth century and culminated in the great exilic prophets Jeremiah, Ezekiel, and 'Deutero-Isaiah' two centuries later. He was apparently well known to the court of King Jeroboam at Samaria, as well as to the religious hierarchies at Bethel, Gilgal, and Beersheba. Like other prophets too, Amos claimed to have seen the Lord (7: 2–3; 9: 1; cf. 3: 7), while the vision-reports in chapters 7–8 confirm that, like them, his prophetic mission was rooted in actual religious experience 'in the days of Uzziah king of Judah and in the days of Jeroboam the son of Joash, king of Israel, two years before the earthquake' (1: 1).

Obadiah

Obadiah was traditionally identified with the champion of Yahwism mentioned in 1 Kings 18: 3 ('now Obadiah revered the Lord greatly') and therefore like Jonah included in the first six Minor Prophets, those from the Assyrian period. The book presupposes a situation of Edomite persecution and violence which can reasonably be identified with the early years of the Babylonian Exile (cf. Jer. 49: 7–22; Ezek. 25: 12–14; Lam. 4: 21–2; Ps. 137: 7–9), but could be applied to any of the countless other periods of crisis down the centuries. The vision that came to Obadiah in such tragic circumstances thus speaks volumes to the hearts of suffering people in every age, expressing their understandable thirst for vengeance and their longing for peace:

> Saviours shall go up to Mount Zion to rule Mount Esau;
> and the kingdom shall be the Lord's
>
> (v. 21)

Jonah

Jonah is one of the twelve Minor Prophets, and not therefore to be grouped, as he often is, with Ruth as a short story or piece of moral instruction. The hero of the book is in fact mentioned in 2 Kings 14: 25 as a contemporary of Amos, living during the prosperous reign of Jeroboam II (*c.*786–746 BC). He is therefore one of the eighth-century prophets and, even although the author of the book lived probably in the fifth century BC, or even later, we must respect his intention, which is to depict Jonah and the other characters in the story as living during the generation leading up to the massive Assyrian invasions of Israel and the destruction of Samaria.

The other preliminary point to remember is that the closest parallels to Jonah are to be found, not in short stories or moral instruction, but in the biographies of the prophets, especially Jeremiah and Elijah. The main theme of the book is the close, almost impertinent relationship between the lonely man of God and his heavenly Master. We may compare Elijah in 1 Kings 19, and Jeremiah in Jer. 20: 'O Lord, you have deceived me!'.

The first question raised by the book is: why did he run away and so flagrantly disobey God's command? There are two answers, bearing in mind what we have just been saying about the setting of the book. In the first place, it is not at all uncommon to hear of a prophet at first finding it hard to obey God's command. Think of Moses (Exod. 3) and Jeremiah (1: 6), for instance. But in the second place, when we place Jonah in his historical setting, we see another reason: he was being asked in effect to sign his own people's death warrant. If he obeyed God, the Assyrians, whose capital was in Nineveh until 612 BC, might repent and be saved, thereby having the chance to invade Israel and destroy it. With prophetic insight, Jonah saw this all too clearly and, torn between loyalty to his people and obedience to his God—a situation prophets frequently find themselves in—he ran away.

Then there is the question of whether the big fish was an instrument of God's judgement or a means of salvation. It is clear from the text that it is the latter: just as the ravens are sent by God to provide Elijah with a means of salvation (1 Kgs. 17), so the big fish is sent to rescue Jonah from drowning. The word used makes this absolutely certain: it is not a monster of the deep, for which there are many names (Rahab, Leviathan, etc.), but a friendly, homely fish. Actually the feminine form is used once (Jonah 2: 1), which probably indicates the author's intention. The rabbis picked this nuance up and added some details to the story: there was a pearl in the belly of the fish to give poor Jonah some light, and the eyes of the fish were like windows through which Jonah could view 'the roots of the mountains' (cf. 2: 6). The psalm in chapter 2 may or may not be by the same author, but it is a very moving testimony to the seriousness of the lonely prophet's plight. He is not a figure of fun, ridiculed for his exclusivist, anti-gentile attitudes, as has so often been maintained, but a lonely suffering servant of God, bewildered by the ways of God.

The climax of the book is the repentance of the citizens of Nineveh (cf. Matt. 12: 41; Luke 11: 32), much to the amazement and horror of Jonah, and the argument of God that, if Jonah is sorry for a plant that grows up over night and dies next day, how much more will God be concerned for the fate of the Ninevites? Jonah is being asked to have compassion for the people of Assyria: this is not just a question of 'preaching to the gentiles'. The Assyrians represent Israel's most barbaric and savage enemies, comparable with the technicians who ran the gas chambers of Auschwitz and Treblinka. So this is an appeal to the reader to consider showing mercy and compassion to his own worst and most irredeemable enemies; and it is appropriate as the text at the centre of the Yom Kippur (Day of Atonement) liturgy, of which the theme is repentance, soul-searching, and newness of life.

Micah

Micah is the last of the six 'Assyrian period' prophets. No biographical details have been recorded except that, like his contemporary Isaiah, he was a Judaean. His home town Moresheth was probably situated somewhere north-west of Hebron; and Jerusalem, Zion, Bethlehem, the Temple, and other Judaean themes take up much of the book. One of the most celebrated prophecies occurs in both Isa. 2: 2–5 and Mic. 4: 1–4. Like Isaiah, too, he turns his attention towards Samaria in the north, e.g.:

> For you have kept the statutes of Omri,
> and all the works of the house of Ahab;

and you have walked in their counsels ...
so you shall bear the scorn of the peoples.
(6: 16; cf. 1: 2–7)

Probably, like Amos, he prophesied mainly against Samaria, recognizing there a cautionary tale of crime and punishment, as that affluent and godless city fell to Assyrian invaders in 721 BC. But, again like the book of Amos, the book of Micah in its present form is addressed to a Judaean audience, at a time when they too had been punished for their sins, and in penitence, were looking for a happier future.

The book is constructed on the same principles as Isaiah 1–12 (p. 39), each biting prophecy of judgement (1: 2–2: 11, chapter 3, and 6: 1–7: 7) capped by a promise of restoration, e.g.:

I will surely gather all of you, O Jacob,
    I will gather the remnant of Israel;
I will set them together
    like sheep in a fold,
like a flock in its pasture,
    a noisy multitude of men.
    (2: 12; cf. chapters 4–5; 7: 8–20).

References, like the one just quoted, to the gathering together of the remnant of Israel (cf. 4: 7) and the rebuilding of the walls of Jerusalem (7: 11) suggest that the book, as we have it, was composed during the Babylonian Exile. But this by no means rules out the possibility that some of the prophecies of salvation go back to the prophet himself, e.g.:

But you, O Bethlehem Ephrathah,
    who are little to be among the clans of Judah,
from you shall come forth for me
    one who is to be ruler in Israel.

(5: 2)

After all, such a Judaean tradition, especially one from so near Micah's home town, arises out of faith in a dynasty that goes back long before Micah. The same applies to the Zion prophecy in chapter 4 (cf. Isa. 2: 2–4).

Many of Micah's prophecies are bitter attacks on social and religious evils. References to false prophets, who prophesy love and peace to earn a living (3: 5), remind us of the traditional suffering role of Israel's prophets, and their courage to preach doom and destruction, if this is the word of God, whatever the consequences for themselves:

> The seers shall be disgraced,
>   and the diviners put to shame;
> they shall all cover their lips,
>   for there is no answer from God.
> But as for me, I am filled with power,
>   with the Spirit of the Lord,
> and with justice and might,
> to declare to Jacob his transgression
>   and to Israel his sin.   (3: 7–8)

Even in the prophecies of hope, there are ferocious, vengeful attacks on the enemies of God (e.g. 7: 15–17). But at the heart of Micah's teaching stands a choice between ritual—'shall I give my first-born for my transgression?' (6: 7)—and what the Lord really requires of us:

> . . . to do justice, and to love kindness,
>   and to walk humbly with your God.   (6: 8)

Nahum

Nahum is the first of three Minor Prophets associated with the decline and fall of the Assyrian Empire, in the reign of Josiah, king of Judah (640–609 BC; cf. Zeph. 1: 1). This was a time of high hopes in Judah, sparked off by the death of the last great king of Assyria, Ashurbanipal (688–627 BC), and the fall of Nineveh, the Assyrian capital, in 612 BC. A reference in 3: 8 to the fall of the Egyptian city No-Ammon (= Thebes), which we know took place in 661, gives us the earliest date for the prophecy of Nahum, but it is probable that it comes from a time much closer to the fall of Nineveh. Satisfaction that Assyrian oppression is nearing its end alternates with confidence that 'the Lord is good, a stronghold in the day of trouble (1: 7) . . . for the Lord is restoring the majesty of Jacob as the majesty of Israel . . .' (2: 2).

Apart from his approximate dates nothing is known of Nahum of Elkosh. Ancient tradition believed he was a Galilean, though any connection with Capernaum (= 'village of Nahum') is without historical foundation, as is the location of his tomb near Nineveh. Verbal links with 1 Kings 11: 39 (cf. 1: 12), Jer. 30: 8 (cf. 1: 13), and Isa. 52: 7 (cf. 1: 15), as well as the insertion of a psalm in chapter 1 (cf. Isa. 12; Jon. 2; Hab. 3), set the book in the mainstream of the prophetic tradition.

The main section consists of a magnificent poem on the fall of Nineveh (chaps. 2–3), comparable with the Song of Deborah (Judg. 5) in its vivid imagery and dramatic power. The size and wealth of the city, richly illumined by the discoveries of nineteenth and twentieth-century archaeologists, provide a magnificent back-drop for the drama, e.g.:

> Nineveh is like a pool
>   whose waters run away.
> 'Halt! Halt!' they cry;
>   but none turns back.
> Plunder the silver,
>   plunder the gold!
> There is no end of treasure,
>   or wealth of every precious thing,   (2: 8–9)

Repeated use of the images of fire and water heightens the effect, and ignominious defeat is expressed in the humiliation of princes, the degradation of the womenfolk, the killing of their children, and the collapse of the city's splendid defences. There is almost nothing religious in this bloodthirsty poem apart from a few hints that the prime mover is God (2: 1, 13; 3: 5–6). The effect of chapter 1, however, is to transform the book into a prophecy about God's justice, and the faith and security of 'those who take refuge in him' (1: 7):

Behold, on the mountains the feet of him
    who brings good tidings,
    who proclaims peace!
Keep your feasts, O Judah,
    fulfil your vows,
for never again shall the wicked come against you,
       he is utterly cut off. (1: 15)

Habakkuk

Like Nahum, Habakkuk probably lived during the reign of Josiah (640–609), and his words reflect the national confidence in Judah during the years leading up to the fall of Nineveh in 612. Nothing is known of his personal life, although we are given two rare glimpses into the prophetic consciousness. The first describes the excitement and anticipation that precedes the moment of revelation:

I will take my stand to watch,
    and station myself on the tower,
and look forth to see what he will say to me ... (2: 1–3)

The second, recalling Isaiah 21 and Jeremiah 20, describes the spiritual turmoil of a man in the throes of prophetic experience (3: 16). To these we may add the reasonable assumption that he was a priest, and the celebrated apocryphal legend that it was Habakkuk who answered Daniel's cry for help from the lions' den (Bel and the Dragon = Dan. 14: 33–9).

The words of this striking figure have been arranged most effectively to convey a sense of progression from lament (1: 1–4) to thanksgiving (chap. 3). Within this framework are contained a beautiful oracle (1: 5–11), a complaint (1: 12–17), the prophet's call (2: 1–5), and a series of judgement prophecies in the traditional 'Woe-form' (2: 6–20). Most of these six units are composed in more or less stereotyped form. The pattern lament + oracle (1: 2–11) belongs to temple ritual, and may suggest that Habakkuk was a cultic prophet (see p. 23), a view perhaps confirmed by the cultic formulas at the beginning and end of chapter 3.

The brilliant imagery of chapter 3 has a long literary history, going back to pre-Israelite Canaan where Resheph (RSV 'pestilence' in v. 5) was a god of plague, and also to the earliest traditions of Yahwism, found in the Song of Deborah (Judg. 5: 4–5) and the Blessing of Moses (Deut. 33: 2):

> God came from Teman,
>   and the Holy One from Mount Paran.
> His glory covered the heavens,
>   and the earth was full of his praise.   (3: 3)

An intriguing illustration of the later history of Habakkuk's words is the grammatically difficult phrase at the end of 3: 8, which has been interpreted as an early reference to Merkabah ('chariot') mysticism: 'Your chariot is salvation' (see pp. 104–5).

In Christian tradition Habakkuk is remembered for a proverb, quoted twice by Paul (Rom. 1: 17; Gal. 3: 11; cf. Heb. 10: 38–9) and central to the theology of Martin Luther: 'But the righteous shall live by his faith' (2: 4).

Zephaniah

Zephaniah, although appearing last of the three prophets associated with the reign of Josiah (1: 1), was probably the earliest. Tradition makes him a contemporary of Jeremiah (1: 1–2) and Huldah (2 Kgs. 22), active like him in the years leading up to Josiah's reformation in 622. Unlike Nahum and Habakkuk, he attacks idolatry (1: 4–6) and arrogance (3: 1–5) among his own people. Possibly international unrest in 627, when the last great king of Assyria, Ashurbanipal, died, inspired some of the Day of the Lord imagery. Nothing else is known of Zephaniah, unless we can deduce, from the long pedigree (including a certain Hezekiah) with which the book opens, that he was a man of aristocratic descent, if not actually a member of the royal family.

The book contains two lengthy prophecies, a spectacular Day of the Lord poem (1: 2–18), and a battery of prophecies of judgement, moving in sequence round the nations of the world from Philistines to Assyrians before settling finally upon Judah (3: 1–7) (see p. 38). The bitter attacks are softened, however, in two ways, possibly by an exilic author. First, a series of moving appeals runs through the book, calling for silence in the presence of the Lord God (1: 7), humility (2: 3), and patience (3: 8):

> Seek the Lord, all you humble of the land,
>   who do his commands;
> seek righteousness, seek humility;
>   perhaps you may be hidden
>   on the day of the wrath of the Lord.   (2: 3)

Secondly, the conclusion (3: 8–20) envisages a time when the whole world will be consumed and a new age will dawn, when the lame and the outcasts will be saved (3: 19).

Out of this colourful little book, it was the horrific Day of the Lord imagery, however, that left its mark on Christian tradition, in the medieval Dies Irae hymn. This was sung at mass on All Souls' Day and at other times in the Western Church till modern times: 'The day of wrath, that day will reduce the earth to ashes ... The trumpet will send its marvellous sound through all the tombs of the earth ...'

Haggai

Haggai, Zechariah, and Malachi are the only prophets that reflect the post-exilic period of restoration. According to Jewish tradition they together founded the Great Synagogue (Aboth 1: 1). With them the age of prophecy is said to have ended, and the Holy Spirit to have departed from Israel. In Christian tradition they similarly represent the climax of the Prophets and point immediately towards fulfilment in the Gospels. Haggai and Zechariah are also associated with the rebuilding of the Temple at Jerusalem, completed in 515 BC, and unique in the instant response to their prophecy and the success of their mission (cf. Hag. 1: 12; Ezra 5: 1–2). The true reason, however for the rebuilding of the Temple in the early years of the reign of Darius the Great (521–495) was probably the sheer might of Persian backing for the project (cf. Ezra 6: 6–12). Thus the role of Haggai

may rather have been to call for a new spirit to revive the community (2: 5), and to point beyond the stones and mortar of the
earthly building to a day when 'the latter splendour of this house
shall be greater than the former', (2: 9) and heaven and earth will
be shaken and the throne of kingdoms overthrown (cf. 2: 21 ff.).
Neither the new building nor the figure of Zerubbabel, Davidic
governor of Judah (Matt. 1: 12), can in reality have been much of
an inspiration to the threatened community at that time. In fact
Zerubbabel disappears from the scene almost immediately, as
though the Persian authorities have removed him as politically
dangerous, and two other generations passed before the city of
Jerusalem was rebuilt (cf. Neh. 2: 11-20).

Haggai's vision is thus one of a God appearing in his glory (1:
8), his spirit dwelling among his people (2: 5; Exod. 25: 8; Rev.
21: 3). He envisages too a temple not built with wood and stones
but with 'the treasures of all nations' (2: 7), and a Messianic age
about to dawn (2: 21-3). He also teaches that moral purity is a
fragile thing, easily crushed by uncleanness (2: 11-14), but without it there can be no future (2: 15-19). While later rabbinic
traditions attributed to Haggai a number of halakhic decisions,
Christian tradition, possibly looking beyond the literal meaning to
the spirit of the text, found in 2: 7 a prophecy of the coming of
Christ, and prescribed the passage to be read in Advent: 'and I
will shake all nations, so that the treasures of all nations shall come
in, and I will fill this house with splendour, says the Lord of
hosts'.

Zechariah

Zechariah's evident interest in the Temple and its liturgy, and the
name of his father Iddo, which appears in a list of priests returning
with the exiles (Neh. 12: 4, 16), suggest that he was himself a
priest as well as a prophet. This assumption and his involvement
in the rebuilding of the Temple (Ezra 5: 1-2) are all we know of
Zechariah. Like Haggai he calls for a right spirit among his
people. The eight visions which make up most of the first chapters
of the book (1-8) are set in a moral framework of appeals to
repent, to obey the Lord, to be silent, to love peace and truth,

and the like, e.g. 'Return to me, says the Lord of hosts, and I will return to you, says the Lord of hosts' (1: 3; cf. 2: 13; 6: 13; 8: 16, 19).

In the first vision, which is reminiscent of Isaiah 6 and 40: 1–8, Zechariah is drawn into conversation with the angels and commissioned to speak 'gracious and comforting words' to his people (1: 7–17). Three of the subsequent visions focus on the two leaders, Zerubbabel 'the Branch' (of David's family tree, that is) and Joshua the High Priest. In chapter 4 these two 'anointed ones' are symbolized as two olive trees on either side of a seven-branched candlestick, and in chapter 6 they are pictured as reigning together in peace and security. Like Haggai, Zechariah sees beyond the human agents and beyond the earthly Temple to heavenly realities beyond, e.g. 'Not by might, nor by power, but by my Spirit, says the Lord of hosts. What are you, O great mountain? Before Zerubbabel you shall become a plain . . . (4: 6–7).

These chapters are full of angels (Satan among them: 3: 2), horses, chariots, horns, mountains, and other symbols, more at home in the apocalyptic style of Daniel and Revelation than among the Prophets, not to mention the flying scroll and the woman in the ephah in chapter 5.

The prophecies in chapters 7–8, dated two years later, present a marvellous picture of the new age:

Thus says the Lord: I will return to Zion, and will dwell in the midst of Jerusalem, and Jerusalem shall be called the faithful city, and the mountain of the Lord of hosts, the holy mountain. Thus says the Lord of hosts: Old men and old women shall again sit in the streets of Jerusalem, each with staff in hand for very age. And the streets of the city shall be full of boys and girls playing in its streets. Thus says the Lord of hosts: If it is marvellous in the sight of the remnant of this people in these days, should it also be marvellous in my sight, says the Lord of hosts? Thus says the Lord of hosts; Behold, I will save my people from the east country and from the west country; and I will bring them to dwell in the midst of Jerusalem; and they shall be my people and I will be their God, in faithfulness and in righteousness. (8: 3–8.)

With masterly originality the author sets this prophecy in the context of a discussion about fasting, so that questions at the beginning of chapter 7 as to whether to mourn and fast on the ninth of Ab (the day the Temple was destroyed) are answered at the end of chapter 8, by the prophecy that all fasts will be transformed in the new age into 'seasons of joy and gladness, and cheerful feasts; therefore love peace and truth' (8: 19).

The second part of Zechariah (9–14) contains none of the recurring motifs of the first part. There are no visions, no angels, no references to Zerubbabel and Joshua or the rebuilding of the Temple, no ethical teaching, no dates. Instead we have a dazzling collection of prophecies on world peace, the deliverance of Jerusalem, and the ingathering of the nations, with the painful corollary that requires the defeat and suffering of Judah's enemies. There is every indication that these chapters come from a period long after the heady optimism of the days of Zerubbabel had passed. The split between Jews and Samaritans, which had taken place by the end of the fourth century, seems to underlie 11: 14. 9: 3–4 most probably alludes to the memorable siege of Tyre by Alexander the Great in 332, while the reference to Greece in verse 13 and the two world powers symbolized by Egypt and Assyria in 10: 10–11 also point to the last years of the fourth century BC. This was a time when the whole world had been rocked by the victories of Alexander and the upheavals that followed his death in 323.

In such a context new images, new ways of thinking evolved. It is here for example that we meet the picture of a king who comes to Jerusalem 'humble and riding on an ass, on a colt the foal of an ass' (9: 9), and the enigmatic prophecy about a compassionate, mourning people: 'And I will pour out on the house of David and the inhabitants of Jerusalem a spirit of compassion and supplication, so that, when they look on him whom they have pierced, they shall mourn for him, as one mourns for an only child, and weep bitterly over him, as one weeps over a first-born' (12: 10–11).

The whole book is filled with allusions to earlier prophetic tradition; and there is no question but that Zechariah stands in the mainstream of biblical prophecy. From the call to repentance in 1: 3 to the 'earthquake in the days of Uzziah king of Judah' in 14:

5 (cf. Amos 1: 1), he is a traditionalist. The book is rich in Messianism too, both the hopes and images associated with Zerubbabel and Joshua in the first six chapters, and the vision of a Messianic era in 7–14. Like Daniel, Joel, and the author of Isaiah 24, Zechariah helps to bridge the gap between prophecy and apocalyptic (p. 89).

Malachi

Malachi in the title is not necessarily a personal name: it means 'my messenger' and occurs also at the beginning of chapter 3. So nothing whatever is known of the author of this little collection of prophecies, probably not even his name. There is some sense, as so often, in the ancient tradition that he was Ezra, a prophet according to the apocryphal 2 Esdras 1: 1. In the first place, references to Temple rituals and mixed marriages suggest a date in the first half of the fifth century BC, close to that of Ezra. Secondly the question–answer form of the prophecies is unique, recalling rabbinic argument rather than traditional prophecy. The verse which relates the prophet's words to the 'law of my servant Moses' (4: 4) is also suggestive, and finally the Elijah prophecy at the end became central to the Pharisaic Judaism which Ezra is traditionally credited with founding. At the least we can say that Malachi prophesied in the years leading up to the reforms of Ezra and Nehemiah and, in some ways, represents the transition from prophecy to Torah scholarship and rabbinic theology.

The heart of the message of the last of the prophets is a traditional, and one might say Deuteronomic, call for a change of heart (cf. Jer. 31: 31–2; Deut. 30: 6). Levi is held up as a model of the covenant relationship (cf. Deut. 33: 8 ff.). There are numerous verbal echoes too, such as 'your eyes shall see . . .' (1: 5; cf. Deut. 4: 3, 10: 21), 'special possession' (3: 17; cf. Deut. 4: 20; 7: 6), 'I have loved you, says the Lord' (1: 2; cf. Deut. 7: 8), and the like. But he breaks new ground in two ways. In addition to the calls for reform among his own people, there is a truly remarkable statement on the worship of other nations: 'For from the rising of the sun to its setting my name is great among the nations, and in every place incense is offered in my name, and a pure offering'

(1: 11). The text as it stands claims that the worship of a righteous idolater is preferable to that of immoral worshippers at the Temple in Jerusalem (vv. 12–14). This goes far beyond Samuel (1 Sam. 15: 22–3) and the eighth-century prophets (e.g. Isa. 1: 10 ff.; Amos 5: 22 ff.). Jewish interpreters, such as the medieval poet and philosopher Solomon ibn Gabirol, made much of this verse as a powerful statement of universalism. Christians drew back from this and understood the verse to refer to a future age when perfect worship would be offered to God.

The other contribution of Malachi to Jewish and Christian tradition is the doctrine of the coming of the messenger to prepare the way of the Lord. The word 'messenger' in 3: 1b is probably to be understood as 'the angel of the Lord' in the ancient sense of God himself in human form, as in his appearance to Moses (Exod. 3: 2), Gideon (Judg. 6: 11–12), and others. But the new emphasis in Malachi, one which was to have a profound influence on Jewish and Christian Messianism, is on the messenger that is to precede the coming of the Lord (3: 1; 4: 5). The last words of Malachi give us the details: he is named as Elijah, the mysterious prophet who appeared on the scene like a *deus ex machina* (1 Kgs. 17: 1) and then 'went up by a whirlwind into heaven' (2 Kgs. 2: 11). His task is to provoke a change of heart in his people, a task to which all the prophets were called. Thus the Prophets end with Moses and Elijah, looking forward to 'the great and terrible day of the Lord' (4: 5) and that change of heart which alone can rescue them from hell-fire. Christians saw in John the Baptist the fulfilment of this final prophecy (Matt. 17: 1–14; Mark 9: 2–13). Jews to this day keep a place for Elijah at every Passover celebration, hoping that he will come to solve all problems (see p. 78) and herald the advent of the Messiah.

7

Prophecy and Interpretation

WE have frequently had occasion to comment on the timelessness of biblical prophecy, its forward-looking dimension, and the role of prophetic legends in later Jewish and Christian tradition. Elijah became the solver of Talmudic puzzles (see p. 78). The suffering servant in Isaiah 53 came to be identified with Christ. The ox and the ass at the beginning of the book of Isaiah appear on our Christmas cards. It is the nature of prophetic literature and indeed of the Bible as a whole that this phenomenon be given some emphasis if we are not to leave the texts in the dusty context of the ancient Near East, surrounded by uncertainties and probabilities. What Isaiah actually meant when he first uttered the words of the Immanuel prophecy (7: 14) will always remain a matter of probabilities. It will also be largely a matter of historical interest. But how his words were understood by Christians down the ages can be established with a fair degree of certainty and objectivity and, what is more, can readily be shown to have had the deepest possible influence on Christian theology and Church history ever since. The fact is that later interpretations of the Prophets, Jewish, Christian, and Muslim, right down to the present day, have gone far beyond the biblical sources themselves, looking for hidden meanings and allusions and devising ingenious methods of exegesis relating the texts to their own experience and bringing them alive in their own day. It is this dimension of biblical prophecy that we shall be examining in the final chapter.

Prophecy and fulfilment in the Bible and the early Church

As we saw, the main criterion for distinguishing true prophecy from false in biblical tradition is fulfilment. This view of the nature of prophecy is not confined to the Mosaic law in Deuteronomy 18. It is clear from that passage, from the historical books Joshua to Kings and 1 and 2 Chronicles, and from numerous passages in the prophetic literature itself, that the argument from prophecy was a major expression of faith in God. Isa. 55: 10–11 is perhaps the best statement:

> For as the rain and the snow come down from heaven,
>   and return not thither but water the earth,
> making it bring forth and sprout,
>   giving seed to the sower and bread to the eater,
> so shall my word be that goes forth from my mouth;
>   it shall not return to me empty,
> but it shall accomplish that which I purpose,
>   and prosper in the thing for which I sent it.

Ezekiel 12 contains another example in which the prophet answers the people's doubts by arguing that fulfilment is imminent:

Son of man, what is this proverb that you have about the land of Israel, saying, 'The days grow long, and every vision comes to naught'? Tell them therefore, 'Thus says the Lord God: I will put an end to this proverb, and they shall no more use it as a proverb in Israel.' But say to them, 'The days are at hand, and the fulfilment of every vision'.   (Ezek. 12: 22–3.)

Of course, without actual fulfilment, without the hard evidence of experience, such prophetic claims seldom convince. Arguments from experience, therefore, after the event, when the words of the prophets have been fulfilled for all to see, are crucial. The passionate conviction that a prophecy will be fulfilled very soon (e.g. Ezek. 12) or at the end of time (e.g. Dan. 12) is one thing; the fact that it has been is a different matter altogether. Let us look at some examples.

In the first place, the whole structure of Israel's history is presented, both in Joshua–Kings and in Chronicles, in such a way as to highlight this phenomenon. The fate of cities, for example, is meticulously related to prophecy (e.g. Josh. 6: 26; cf. 1 Kgs. 16: 34; 2 Chr. 36: 21). Needless to say, literary invention is an integral part of this process. It was easy to insert the story of an unnamed prophet appearing on the scene and predicting an event some time later (e.g. 1 Kgs. 13: 1–10; cf. 2 Kgs. 16: 23), or to adjust such details as the date in order to match prophecy and fulfilment more perfectly (e.g. Isa. 7: 8). On the other hand, an event could be invented or at least elaborately embroidered to match a well-documented prophecy that was already in existence. This is what happened in the case of the return of the exiles in Ezra 1–2. One reason why the author of that passage presents us with the totally unhistorical picture of 42,360 exiles besides their servants of whom there were 7,337, plus 200 male and female singers, returning to Jerusalem and Judah each to his own town (Ezra 2: 1, 64–5), is that he wanted to show how prophecies like Isa. 51: 11 were fulfilled, even if they had not been:

> And the ransomed of the Lord shall return,
>   and come to Zion with singing
>   everlasting joy shall be upon their heads . . .

Perhaps the frequent mention of 'singers' (Ezra 2: 41, 65, 70; 3: 10–11) among the returning exiles alludes to this and other Isaianic prophecies (cf. 51: 3; 52: 8–9; 54: 1–3; 55: 12), and the reference to the exclusion of unclean priests (Ezra 2: 62–3) is linked to Isa. 52: 11:

> Depart, depart, go out thence,
>   touch no unclean thing;
> go out from the midst of her, purify yourselves,
>   you who bear the vessels of the Lord.

The Ezra passage illustrates the power of prophecy to create its own fulfilment in spite of the evidence. Haggai also saw beyond the same facts to glories that transcend them (e.g. 2: 9). These are theological statements expressing faith in God, whatever happens.

Another popular device is the attribution to an ancient prophet of prophecies concerning events that have recently occurred or are actually unfolding in the author's own day. Thus in eighth-century BC Samaria Amos was able to prophesy that Jerusalem would be rebuilt after the Babylonian Exile, and Isaiah from eighth-century BC Jerusalem predicted with the same accuracy events that took place 200 years later, such as the appearance of Cyrus on the international scene (44: 28; 45: 1), the presence of Jews in Syene in Upper Egypt (49: 12), and the fall of Babylon (47: 1).

Daniel 11 provides an even more spectacular example in which a prophet living in sixth-century BC Babylon foretells in massive detail the events leading up to and including the Maccabean crisis of 168–164 BC (cf. p. 114). By substituting ciphers for actual names (e.g. 'king of the south' for Ptolemy; 'king of the north' for Antiochus; 'Kittim' for the Romans in 11: 30) the author heightens the mysterious effect of Daniel's prophecy, as do the repeated references to his extraordinary visionary experiences (e.g. 8: 27; chap. 10). The tense in such prophecies remains in the future, but fulfilment is implied by the author who deliberately matches the prophet's words to historical events, familiar to his readers. The purpose is the same as in the simpler examples: he is declaring that history is controlled by God, and that he reveals his will to his prophets. In the words of an earlier prophet:

> Surely the Lord God does nothing,
> without revealing his secret
> to his servants the prophets.   (Amos 3: 7)

The traditional division of the Christian Bible into an 'Old Testament' and a 'New Testament' has tended to break the continuity that manifestly exists there, from the first book to the last, from the vision of the prophet Moses in the Pentateuch to the vision of John of Patmos in the book of Revelation. The 'Old/New' division also suggests a relationship between the two parts, not only of prophecy and fulfilment, but of supersession, with the risk of damaging consequences for Christian perceptions of the 'Old' parts of scripture, and, regrettably, of Jews and Judaism. Continuity might be better expressed by grouping Isaiah, known to Christians since early times as the 'Fifth Gospel', and the other Prophets, with the Gospels and Paul, rather than with the Pentateuch, Historical Books, Psalms and Wisdom. Texts providing scriptural authority for the Virgin Birth (Isa. 7: 14), the Suffering Messiah (Isa. 53), the Mission to the Gentiles (Isa. 49: 6), the New Covenant (Jer. 31: 31) and countless other fundamental Christian beliefs, appear already in the Prophets.

In addition to the arrangement of the books, pointing upwards and forwards to fulfilment (see p. 1), a further expression of this continuity is the custom, so well documented in the later books of scripture, of Christian writers and preachers to use passages from the earlier books to give authority to what they are saying, or to explain it or give it some added effect. This imposes a structure upon the whole Christian Bible, exactly parallel to that of the so-called Deuteronomic history (Joshua–Kings) discussed in the previous section. Integral to that structure is the element of prophecy and fulfilment.

Two routes led to this use of scripture. Some passages were read and interpreted regularly in Jewish homes and synagogues, and must have become familiar throughout the Jewish world. In such cases the question was: what does this mean? or when is this prophecy going to be fulfilled? Luke 4: 16–21 seems to be an example. Jesus is given the book of Isaiah and, in response to the congregation's questioning looks, he explains what it means: 'Today this scripture has been fulfilled in your hearing'. This type of exegesis starts from the text, and seeks to explain its meaning in such a way as to make it come alive for contemporary readers or listeners. It occurs in commentaries, such as the Jewish Midrashic literature, and the *pesher* literature from Qumran (cf. p. 150), and in homilies based on a lectionary. But it is rare in the early Church.

Early Christian writers normally use scripture in a quite different way. Their object is seldom to discuss the meaning of a text. They wish only to use it as a vehicle to express their own beliefs or describe their own experiences. Instead of working through the books of the Bible, commenting on the continuous texts, they 'search the scriptures' (John 5: 39) to discover isolated texts to build into their narrative or discourse. Thus, for example, in Matthew 1, Isa. 7: 14 is divorced from its context in the book of Isaiah and applied to the birth of Jesus, not because the author has been wondering what it meant, but because it expresses his belief that (1) Jesus was born of a virgin, (2) in Jesus 'God is with us'

(= Immanuel) in a special way, and (3) the coming of Jesus is a fulfilment of prophecy. In its original context the woman is not described as a virgin (unless Matthew knew only the Greek translation which he quotes), and the prophecy is one of judgement not salvation. But, taken out of context, it is a marvellously rich prophecy of the coming of Jesus Christ, and has functioned as such in Christian tradition ever since.

Place-names provide an easy point of contact between Scripture and contemporary events. Thus Mic. 5: 2 speaks of Bethlehem as the future birthplace of a Davidic Messiah and so provides an ideal expression of the author's belief that Christ was born there (Matt. 2: 6). The same applies to his use of Isa. 9: 1, which originally referred to the Assyrian invasions of northern Israel, in 734–732 BC, but is brilliantly applied to the appearance of Jesus in Nazareth, Capernaum, and other parts of Galilee (Matt. 4: 12–16). Many other details in the story of the life of Jesus are described in this way: e.g. riding into Jerusalem on an ass (Zech. 9: 9; Matt. 21: 5; John 12: 15); Judas's thirty pieces of silver (Zech. 11: 12–13; Matt. 26: 15; 27: 9); the piercing of Jesus' side (Zech. 12: 10; John 19: 27). The teaching of Jesus is similarly presented as 'fulfilling' Scripture: e.g. the cleansing of the Temple (Jer. 7: 11; Matt. 21: 13); his attacks on hypocrisy (Isa. 29: 13; Matt. 15: 8–9). The Psalms of David are often used in this way, especially because, for the early Christian writers, they too are about a Davidic Messiah: e.g. speaking in parables (Ps. 78: 2; Matt. 13: 35); lots cast for his clothing (Ps. 22: 18; John 19: 24); the cry of dereliction on the cross (Ps. 22: 1; Mark 15: 34).

What has been said about the life and teaching of Jesus applies also to theological discussion about him. Thus he is the prophet foretold in Deut. 18: 15–16 (Acts. 3: 17–26); the son of God (Ps. 110: 4; Gen. 14: 17–20; Heb. 5: 6; 7: 1–3); 'the first and the last' (Isa. 48: 12; Rev. 22: 13). The same method is used in the discussion of other doctrines and beliefs as well. For example, Hosea's poignant tale of disloyalty and reconciliation with God's people is applied by Paul to the Gentiles: 'Those who were not my people. I will call "my people", and her who was not beloved, I will call "my beloved"' (Rom. 9: 25). Isa. 65: 1, which had a universalist meaning from the start, is cited in the next chapter

(10: 20). More scriptural authority for such universalist teaching is found by Jesus, rather unexpectedly, in the figures of Elijah and Elisha;

But in truth, I tell you, there were many widows in Israel in the days of Elijah, when the heaven was shut up three years and six months, when there was a great famine over all the land; and Elijah was sent to none of them but only to Zarephath, in the land of Sidon, to a woman who was a widow. And there were many lepers in Israel at the time of the prophet Elisha; and none of them was cleansed, but only Naaman the Syrian (Luke 4: 25–7).

The resurrection of the dead was not a major theme in Scripture: the Sadducees denied it altogether on scriptural grounds. But Paul, firmly within rabbinic tradition, identifies two passages which, whatever their original meaning, he uses to good effect at the conclusion of his discussion of the subject in 1 Cor. 15: 54–5: 'Death is swallowed up in victory' (Isa. 25: 8); 'O death where is thy victory? O death where is thy sting?' (cf. Hos. 13: 14).

The process continues on into the early Church, where not only was scriptural authority sought for every doctrine, but scriptural language and imagery was assumed to be the preferred medium for all Christian teaching. The doctrine of the Trinity, for example, was recognized in the 'Trisagion' ('thrice holy') (Isa. 6: 3): 'Holy, holy, holy is the Lord of hosts'. Isa. 9: 6 confirmed the divinity of Christ, and Isaiah 53 the atoning significance of his death. Isa. 66: 24 (cf. Ecclus. 7: 17 Greek) gives rare biblical authority for hell-fire.

The ox and the ass found their way into the nativity story from Isaiah 1: 3:

> The ox knows its owner,
>   and the ass its master's crib;
> but Israel does not know,
>   my people does not understand.

This readily took on a polemical tone, drawing an invidious comparison—similar to the one the original prophet intended—

between the Jews who did not accept that Jesus was God ('owner ... master') and the dumb animals who did. Isa. 49: 16 foretold the stigmata on Christ's hands, and the enigmatic 'rich man' in Isa. 53: 9 was naturally Joseph of Arimathea; the fourth man who appeared in the burning furnace 'like a son of the gods' (Dan. 3: 25) was understood to be the risen Christ. Details of the shepherd image were drawn from Isa. 40: 11, and invitations like Isa. 55: 1—'Ho, everyone who thirsts'—applied to Christ's invitation to the Last Supper (cf. Isa. 12: 3; Gen. 14: 18; Prov. 9: 5). The canonization of a text means its removal from the context where it originated and its application to the beliefs, stories, and experiences of the living Church.

Two final examples will illustrate how the history of biblical prophecy continued into the early Church. No verse had more impact on the phenomenon than Joel 2: 28 (Hebr. 3: 1) with its prediction that in the new age men and women, young and old, would receive the gift of prophecy. According to Acts, this is what happened, first in Jerusalem at Pentecost (Acts 2), and then later at Ephesus where gentiles first received the gift too (10: 44 ff.). Within the new community certain men and women were recognized as 'prophets' in the sense that, like Stephen, they were 'full of grace and power and did great wonders and signs among the people' (6: 8). Barnabas was another (cf. 11: 24) and Philip (cf. 8: 4–8). Philip's four unmarried daughters are described as prophets too (21: 9), and they provided scriptural inspiration and authority for the second century apocalyptic/ascetic movement founded by Montanus and his two associates Prisca and Maximilla.

Some have argued that Paul himself should be described as a prophet, taking into account his election 'from the womb' (Gal. 1: 15; cf. Isa. 49: 1; Jer. 1: 5), his call (e.g. Acts 9; cf. Ezek. 1–2; Dan. 7: 9 ff.), his heavenly vision (2 Cor. 12: 2–4; cf. Isa. 6; Jer. 23: 18), and the like. He is compared to the biblical prophets, both in Acts (e.g. Acts 13: 47; 8: 26) and in his own writings (e.g. Gal. 1: 15 f.), and perhaps he has himself in mind when he contrasts 'prophetic powers' with the power of love in 1 Corinthians 13.

The Prophets in ancient Judaism

In the mainstream of orthodox Judaism, the Prophets have never attained the same central role as they did in Christianity. An early example of this contrast is to be found in Ben Sira (*c.*180 BC), whose great hymn in praise of famous men from Adam to Nehemiah (Ecclus. 44–9) devotes only a few verses to the Latter Prophets (Isaiah to Malachi), while from the Former Prophets (Joshua–Kings), Samuel, Elijah, and Elisha receive only slightly more extended treatment. The custom of reading portions of the Prophets immediately after the reading of the Torah on sabbaths and feast-days ('haftarahs') goes back to the time of Christ (cf. Luke 4: 17), and the lectionary, for feast days and fasts at any rate, was fixed by the middle of the second century AD. But of the eighty or so relatively short passages thus annually read out and occasionally preached upon, less than half come from the Latter Prophets, twenty from Isaiah and the rest divided equally between Jeremiah (nine), Ezekiel (ten), and the Twelve (fourteen). This means that many passages, like Isaiah 53, familiar to Christians, are much less familiar to the orthodox Jew. There is much less emphasis on the 'Immanuel prophecy' (Isa. 7: 14), for instance, the Messianic hymn in Isa. 9: 1–6 ('the people that walked in darkness have seen a great light'), the Pentecost passage in Joel (2: 28), and all the Zechariah passages cited above as prophecies about Christ (9: 9; 11: 12 ff.; 12: 10). On the other hand, Isaiah's vision in the Temple (Isa. 6), 'Comfort, comfort my people' (Isa. 40: 1–26), the vision in the valley of dry bones (Ezek. 37), Micah's 'What does the Lord require of you . . .' (Mic. 6: 8), and other passages are equally familiar to both.

Telling examples of the Jewish use of the Prophets in the liturgy are the association of Jonah with Yom Kippur, Zechariah's vision of the golden lamp (Zech. 2: 14–4: 7) with Hanukkah (1 Macc. 4: 49–50), Ezekiel's chariot vision (Ezek. 1) with the Sinai theophany (Exod. 18: 1–20: 23) on the first day of the Feast of Weeks, and a powerful selection of Isaianic material (Isa. 10: 33–12: 6) with the last day of the Passover celebrations. The daily Prayer Book draws heavily on the prophetic traditions too: for example the 'Eighteen Benedictions', one of the oldest and best known parts of the daily liturgy, contains prayers for the resurrection of the dead, the rebuilding of Jerusalem, the return of the exiles, and the coming of the Messiah, all in language drawn directly from the Prophets, especially Isaiah. Random verses from the Prophets are cited frequently as proof texts in the Talmud, as though they possess scriptural authority equal to the Torah. A rare reference to Isaiah 53, in a discussion of the concept of a suffering Messiah, will illustrate this: 'Our teachers have said: His name shall be the Leprous One, as it says, "Surely he bore our sicknesses, and carried our pains: yet we esteemed him as one stricken with leprosy, and smitten of God" [Isa. 53: 4]' (Sanh. 98b).

Another indication of the relatively low priority given to the Prophets in Judaism is to be found in the midrashic literature. Of the vast numbers of ancient Jewish commentaries, known as midrashim, only a fraction is devoted to the Prophets. Many midrashim on the Torah, or parts of it, have survived, as also on the Five Scrolls (Ruth, Esther, Song of Songs, Ecclesiastes, and Lamentations) and Psalms, but almost none on the Prophets. Jonah is the one exception, being, like the works just listed, regularly used in the liturgy. For systematic commentaries on the Prophets we have to rely on medieval collections, the best known of which is Yalkut Shimoni, a midrashic thesaurus of the whole of the Hebrew Bible probably composed in Germany in the first half of the thirteenth century. A modern 'yalkut' in English is Louis Ginzberg's *Legends of the Jews*.

There are also the medieval Bible commentaries on the Prophets by Rashi, David Kimhi, and Ibn Ezra, printed in all rabbinic Bibles alongside the biblical text. These are the most widely consulted Jewish commentaries in use today. Like Yalkut Shimoni, they are not available in English, but the Soncino commentaries on the Bible regularly quote them and are helpful. For examples of midrashic comments on the Prophets, see above on Elijah, Jeremiah, Jonah, and Malachi. Finally, the mystical Hekhalot literature takes as its starting-point the 'chariot vision' of Ezekiel 1 (see pp. 104–5), and speculates on such passages as Isaiah 6, but can hardly be described as a systematic commentary on the prophetic literature.

Not until relatively modern times has Judaism discovered the

Prophets. Nearly all the poetry of Bialik (1873–1934) abounds with allusions to the Bible, but especially the Prophets, e.g. 'What is my offence, what is my strength? I am not a poet nor a prophet, but a woodcutter' ('My soul has sunk down'; trans. T. Carmi). The allusion to Amos 7: 14 is very effective. Martin Buber and Avraham Joshua Heschel are two other modern writers whose works on the Prophets broke new ground in the history of Jewish exegesis.

A rich source of information on how Jewish communities in ancient times interpreted the Prophets and applied them to events and conditions in their own experience is translation into the vernacular. Some examples from the Greek translation of the Prophets will illustrate how events in second-century BC Jewish history were related to the prophecies of Isaiah and Amos. Isaiah 19 ends with a remarkable blessing of 'my people Egypt' and, since the Greek version of the Hebrew Bible was produced primarily for the thriving Greek-speaking Jewish community in Egypt, it is no surprise to find that a Greek translator has added the preposition 'in' to change 'my people Egypt', to 'my people in Egypt', thereby redirecting the blessing away from Egypt in general to his own community there. He does a similar thing in 11: 16 and 28: 5, where he adds 'in Egypt' to references to 'the remnant': 'In that day the Lord of hosts will be a crown of hope, and a diadem of glory to the remnant of his people in Egypt' (28: 5 Greek).

Similarly the reference in Isa. 19: 18 to 'the city of the sun' (RSV), a city in Egypt which will 'swear allegiance to the Lord of hosts', was identified with Heliopolis where, according to Josephus (*Antiquities*, 13: 68), Jews believed the exiled High Priest Onias built a New Jerusalem 'as the prophet Isaiah had foretold' (see also p. 151).

Amos 3: 12 illustrates another type of contemporary application: the Greek version alters what was originally a bitter attack on affluent Samaria in the days of Amos into a twofold sectarian assult on his contemporaries: 'As a shepherd pulls out of the mouth of a lion two legs and a piece of an ear, so shall the people of Israel who dwell in Samaria . . . and those priests in Damascus be pulled out' (Amos 3: 12 Greek). The polemical allusions to the

Samaritans and the Zadokite sect, best known to us today from the Dead Sea Scrolls, are unmistakable (cf. Ecclus. 50: 25–6).

The ancient Aramaic versions of the Hebrew Bible, the Targums, go further in the direction of interpreting and explaining the text in terms of the beliefs and circumstances of their own day. Thus, for example, Messianism as it had developed by the first century AD at the very latest has left its mark very strongly on the Targum of Isaiah. The term 'the Messiah' is inserted after 'my servant' in Isa. 52: 13 (also in 53: 10) and the meaning of the poem radically adapted to more conventional Messianic language:

And it was the will of the Lord to refine and purify the remnants of his people in order to cleanse their soul from sins. They shall look upon the kingdom of their Messiah: they shall multiply sons and daughters, they shall prolong days, and those who perform the law of the Lord shall prosper in his good pleasure. (Isa. 53: 10 Targ.)

Notice how much longer the Aramaic version is and how far from the Hebrew text. It comes closer to Daniel (e.g. 11: 32–5) than to the eighth-century prophets. But given that Scripture is intended to speak to every age, then what it originally meant may often have a low priority in the context of a religious community that canonized it.

The Qumran Scrolls provide us with an interesting sample of a sectarian interpretation of the same prophetic texts. Composed for the most part during the last two centuries BC by an ascetic Jewish sect which, like Christianity, broke away from the Jerusalem hierarchy, the Qumran literature includes not only manuscripts of all the books of the Hebrew Bible (except Esther) and many of the Apocryphal works canonized by some branches of the Christian Church (e.g. Enoch), but also a quantity of sectarian writings, commentaries on Scripture, hymns, manuals, laws, and the like, which give us a unique insight into the history, organization, life, and beliefs of an alternative to rabbinic Judaism. Like virtually all other varieties of Judaism, including Christianity, the sect, probably a form of Essenism, was heavily dependent on the Hebrew Bible which its members interpreted by their own distinctive methods and for their own religious purposes. We shall look

briefly at examples from three types of material: biblical manuscripts, especially the complete Isaiah Scrolls; commentaries on
the text, in particular the Habakkuk *pesher*; and other texts,
especially the Damascus Rule, in which isolated biblical texts are
cited and interpreted.

Biblical manuscripts, written about a thousand years before our
other Hebrew manuscripts of the Bible, prove how extraordinarily
successful the Jewish scribes have been in preserving the text of
the Bible almost unchanged for so many centuries. But in some
passages, often where there are difficulties of some kind, they
show how a scribe could choose a reading which agreed with the
beliefs of the sect. In Isa. 19: 18, for example, the reading is 'city
of the sun' instead of the official 'city of destruction' (MT; AV).
'City of the sun' represents opposition to Jerusalem shared both by
the Qumran sect and by Onias, exiled High Priest who founded a
new Jerusalem at Leontopolis in the district of Heliopolis ('city of
the sun'), at about the same time as the Qumran sect broke away
from the Jerusalem hierarchy. A variant reading in Isa. 6: 13 is
another example. By simply spacing the words differently, the
meaning is changed from a prophecy of hope for David's Messianic
descendants in Judah (cf. RSV) to a dismissive question: 'How
could its stump be the holy seed?'

The few *pesher* commentaries that have survived from Qumran
are preoccupied with the fulfilment of prophecy in the experience
of the community, in particular with regard to their escape from
the corrupt hierarchy at Jerusalem and the imminent end of the
present age. In his commentary on Hab. 2: 1–2, for example, the
author explains that God told Habakkuk to write down what would
happen to the final generation ('write down the vision...') and
that 'he who reads it...' refers to the Teacher of Righteousness
(one of the leaders of the community) 'to whom God made known
all the mysteries of the words of His servants the prophets'. The
famous line 'But the righteous shall live by his faith' (2: 4; cf.
Rom. 1: 17) is interpreted as referring to 'all those who observe
the law in the House of Judah, whom God will deliver from the
House of Judgment because of their suffering and because of their
faith in the Teacher of Righteousness'. The subsequent verses,
describing arrogance, greed, and violence, are interpreted as

referring to the 'Wicked Priest' at Jerusalem who 'forsook God and betrayed the precepts for the sake of riches' (on 2: 5), and pursued the Teacher of Righteousness to the house of his exile, where he burst in on the community on the Day of Atonement 'their sabbath of repose' (on 2: 15). In 2: 27 'Lebanon' means the Council of the Community, the 'beasts' are the poor of Judah who keep the law, and the 'city' is Jerusalem where the Wicked Priest committed abominable deeds and defiled the Temple of God (Vermes, *The Dead Sea Scrolls in English*, pp. 235–43).

Sometimes actual historical persons are named: thus the lion in Nahum 2: 11 is interpreted as 'Demetrius, king of Greece', probably Demetrius III Eukairos, king of Syria during the reign of Alexander Jannaeus (103–76 BC) (Josephus, *Antiquities*, 13: 370–8). But normally the 'code names' are left unexplained, perhaps originally because they were well enough known, but later probably because interest was theological rather than historical. Decipherment is a peculiarly modern preoccupation.

The third example of Qumran exegesis comes from a continuous narrative, in which frequent quotations from the Prophets are given and explained. The first part of the Damascus Rule tells the story of how the remnant of Israel escaped from the corruption of Judah and entered into a New Covenant 'in the land of Damascus'. At every stage prophecies are fulfilled; and it is particularly noteworthy how in this process passages originally intended as prophecies of judgement are transformed into prophecies of salvation for the new community. Isa. 7: 17 and Amos 5: 26–7 illustrate this. In the first case, the split in Israel into north and south, when Ephraim departed from Judah, is understood to refer to the time when 'those who held fast escaped to the north and all the apostates were given up to the sword'. The Amos passage develops this line of thought in some detail: 'I will exile the tabernacle of your king and the bases of your statues from my tent to Damascus'. This is interpreted as a prophecy that the Law (tabernacle) and the Prophets (bases of the statues) will one day be taken away from Jerusalem (tent), and entrusted to the congregation (king) and 'the Interpreter of the Law' (star) in the new community (Damascus). Ezek. 45: 15 can readily be interpreted in a similar way, while Hos. 5: 10 contains a particularly vicious and appropriate attack on the 'princes of Judah'. The Qumran sect, like the early Christians, shows a particular fondness for quoting the Prophets. Outspoken criticism of Jerusalem and Judah is another feature common to both Christianity and Qumran.

A final example of Qumran exegesis provides further links with early Christian thinking, in this case in the Epistle to the Hebrews. In a remarkable document, unfortunately badly damaged, Melchizedek (cf. Heb. 7) appears 'at the end of days' as a heavenly saviour figure, proclaiming liberty to the captives and comfort to those who mourn (Isa. 61: 1): 'as it is written concerning him, *who says to Zion: Your ELOHIM reigns* (Isa. 52: 7). *Zion* is . . . those who uphold the Covenant, who turn from walking in the way of the people. And *your ELOHIM* is Melchizedek, who will save them from the hand of Satan' (Vermes, *The Dead Sea Scrolls in English*, pp. 265–8). *ELOHIM* is the Hebrew word for 'God' or 'angels', in such passages as Ps. 8: 4.

Biblical Prophecy in the history of religion

In no sense can we consider Muslim interpretation of scripture as parallel to Jewish and Christian. Muslim tradition denies the authority of the Bible. Their doctrine of *tahrif* 'corruption', according to which Jews altered or corrupted the Scriptures for their own purposes, leads to the conclusion that there is no scripture apart from the Holy Qur'ān. It cannot therefore be said that the Qur'ān interprets the Bible as, for example, scripture is interpreted in the Gospels or the Mishnah. It is of purely academic interest to discuss the relationship between the Qur'ān and the Bible, and to speculate on how it came about that so many familiar stories appear in the Qur'ān in a form quite different from the biblical tradition. In fact it is clear that this is because between the Bible and the Qur'ān at least 600 years of Jewish and Christian exegesis passed, and the Muslim traditions often come closer to this exegesis than to the original biblical texts. But this is of no consequence to Muslim interpreters of the Qur'ān who simply ignore the Bible entirely.

The prophets, however, are central to Islam. They include not only Abraham (cf. Gen. 20: 7), Elijah, Jonah, and other biblical prophets, but also Adam, Noah, Joseph, Job, Aaron, David (cf. also Acts 2: 30), Solomon, and other biblical characters (e.g. Surah 21). There are also several Arabian prophets not mentioned in the Bible, such as Hud, Salih, Shu'aib (identified with Jethro), and Idris (identified with Enoch). Common to most of the Qur'ānic stories of the prophets is the theme of the lonely prophet sent with a message of judgement to his people and rejected by them. We can recognize the early experience of Muhammad in some of these tales as for example in the heart-rending prayers of Noah (Surah 71), e.g.:

My Lord, I have called my people by night and by day but my calling has only increased them in flight. And whenever I called them, that Thou mightest forgive them, they put their fingers in their ears, and wrapped them in their garments, and persisted, and waxed very proud ... My Lord, leave not upon the earth of the unbelievers even one ... (vv. 5–6, 27.)

Pride of place among the Islamic prophets goes to Jesus, son of the virgin Mary, who is called the Messiah, the Word of God, and the Spirit of God. The Qur'ān records the miracle of the clay birds, found also in the gnostic Gospel of Thomas, and, like the docetists, explains that he was not actually crucified, but only appeared to die. His sinlessness and his Second Coming are also referred to. According to a later tradition, based probably on an ingenious reading of John 14: 16, he also foretold the coming of Muhammad.

Finally we come to Muhammad himself, last in the long series of prophets sent by God, 'Seal of the Prophets', 'Messenger of God' *par excellence*. According to the Qur'ān Muhammad made no claims for himself. Like Amos (7: 14–15), he protested that he had no training as a prophet; indeed he was unable to read or write according to Muslim doctrine. What he said was thus the unadulterated word of God, delivered to him by the angels. Nor was he an ecstatic or a poet or a soothsayer. He performed no miracles. His call came to him at the age of 40 in the form of a frightening vision, the first of many that continued till his death twenty-two years later. There is also mention in the Qur'ān of a 'Night-journey' (Surah 17: 1), and on the basis of this grew up an elaborate account of his journey to heaven and back, like that of Paul (2 Cor. 12: 1–4) and Enoch. The original emphasis on the humanity of the Prophet—he is even rebuked for being impatient with a blind beggar who came to him for help (Surah 80)—was inevitably modified as later Muslim writers looked back to him as the founder of their religion, and believers regularly recite his name along with that of God in the *shahada* (confession of faith): 'There is no God but Allah and Muhammad is his prophet.'

This brings us to the two other 'monotheistic' religions, Judaism and Christianity, and we shall conclude by looking briefly at a few examples of popular attempts to identify fulfilled prophecy in their own time: first Jewish, then Christian. We have already seen how in Haggai and Zechariah Messianic hopes were applied to the Davidic leader of the Jewish community, Zerubbabel, at the time of the rebuilding of the Temple, and how soon these hopes were dashed. Traditional Messianic terms like 'Branch', 'anointed', 'servant of the Lord' (Hag. 2: 23), and 'chosen' were then for the first time applied to a living individual. Elsewhere in the prophetic literature, no name is associated with the Messianic vocabulary (except of course David) and it is therefore available for the community or an individual within it to apply to anyone they believe to have fulfilled their Messianic hopes. Jesus of Nazareth is clearly the best documented example of all time, but there are others. The leader of the Second Jewish Revolt under Hadrian (AD 132–5), a man named Simon ben Kosiba, was regarded as the Messiah by many. Among them was Akiba, who believed that the famous Messianic prophecy 'A star (Kokhba) shall go forth from Jacob' (Num. 24: 17) was fulfilled in Ben Kosiba, who was accordingly nicknamed 'Son of the star' (Bar Kokhba) by his followers. The revolt ended in disaster, however, and opponents named him instead Bar Koziba 'Son of the Lie'.

The life and teaching of a later false Messiah, Shabbetai Zevi (1626–76), had repercussions throughout Europe and the Middle

East. Schooled in Talmudic and cabbalistic Judaism (a form of Jewish mysticism) and apparently influenced by the Messianic expectations of various Jewish and Christian groups, Shabbetai at the age of 22 came to believe that he was the Messiah, and sought to convince his followers in Smyrna of this. Within twenty years his name was familiar in synagogues all over the world. His picture appeared in prayer books, showing him enthroned in splendour, the words of Jeremiah printed prominently: 'In those days and at that time I will cause a righteous Branch to spring forth for David: and he shall execute justice and righteousness in the land'. (33: 15). At the beginning of the year 1666 he proclaimed that Zechariah's prophecy was now fulfilled and decreed that the fast of the tenth month (10 Tevet) must be changed into a 'season of joy and gladness' (Zech. 8: 19). But his Messiahship ended in disillusionment. He himself was discredited, first, by an embarrassing confrontation with another 'Messiah', and then by his own conversion to Islam. His followers for the most part admitted their error, to the scornful delight of their opponents, especially Christians.

A third example of how biblical prophecy is used by Jewish communities to express their hopes and ideals is modern Zionism. Settlements were from the beginning given biblical names like Petah Tikva 'the door of hope' (Hos. 2: 15), Mevasseret Zion 'O thou that tellest good tidings to Zion' (Isa. 40: 9), Yish'i 'my salvation' (Isa. 51: 5), and She'ar Yashuv 'a remnant will return' (Isa. 7: 3; 10: 21–2). One of the early Zionist organizations was called 'Bilu' after the first letters of the four Hebrew words translated 'House of Jacob, come, let us walk (in the light of the Lord)' (Isa. 2: 5), and Israel's first airline was called El Al after a phrase in Hos. 11: 7 (AV 'to the most high'). The effect of this remarkable phenomenon on political groupings within Israel and on prospects for peace in the Middle East is incalculable.

Since for Christians prophecies about the coming of the Messiah were fulfilled in Christ, biblical authority for such beliefs as the Second Coming of Christ or the end of the world were sought in the Gospels and Paul rather than the Prophets, in such passages as Matthew 24–5, Mark 13, Luke 21, 1 Thess. 4: 13–18, and other apocalyptic passages. These were dependent on Daniel, Joel,

Zephaniah, and the like (cf. Joel 2: 10–11; Zeph. 1: 15; Dan. 7: 13; Zech. 9: 14).

Dates and numbers, such as those in Daniel, were often used to calculate when Christ would return, as in the case of William Miller (1782–1849), founder of the Adventist sect, who fixed the Second Coming in 1843–4. C. T. Russell (1852–1916), founder of the sect known today as Jehovah's Witnesses, calculated that the Second Coming would take place in 1874, and the end of the world in 1914. The outbreak of a World War in that year convinced many of the truth of his calculations, and his 'Watchtower Bible and Tract Society', founded in 1884, is still flourishing. The title 'watchtower' comes from Hab. 2: 1–3.

Another modern phenomenon that draws heavily upon biblical prophecy is Liberation Theology. The attacks on the rich who oppress the poor (e.g. Amos 2: 6–7; Isa. 10: 1–2) and the demand for justice (e.g. Amos 5: 24; Isa. 1: 17; Mic. 6: 8) speak directly to the plight of the poor in the Third World. Criticism of the religious institutions (e.g. Amos 4: 4–5; Jer. 7: 1–4) has a special relevance there too. If the Son of Man is identified with the poor (cf. Matt. 25: 31–46), then Daniel's vision takes on a whole new meaning (cf. Dan. 7: 14; see p. 117). The 'Church of the poor' can find plenty of powerful statements in its support in biblical prophecy, e.g.:

> The spirit of the Lord God is upon me,
>   because the Lord has anointed me
> to bring good tidings to the poor;
>   he has sent me to bind up the brokenhearted,
> to proclaim liberty to the captives.
>
> (Isa. 61: 1; cf. 58: 6–9)

The Magnificat (Luke 1: 46–55) picks up a number of variations on this theme (e.g. 1 Sam. 2: 1–10) and visualizes a new society where the oppressed are liberated and the hungry satisfied;

> He has shown strength with his arm,
> he has scattered the proud in the imagination of their hearts,

> he has put down the mighty from their thrones...
> and the rich he has sent empty away.
>
> (Luke 1: 51–2)

The setting up of such a new society, with God's help, is identified with an act of creation: we have seen how the liberation of slaves in Egypt and the creation of heaven and earth can be combined in one poem about the cosmic power of God (see p. 50). Amos 4: 5 marvellously contrasts human strength that exults in exploiting the poor with the might of the creator who is a God of justice and righteousness (see pp. 50–1). The vision of a new creation at the end of the book of Isaiah focuses on a just society in which everyone, young and old, will enjoy long and happy lives in security and peace. In what look like allusions to Genesis 3, even the curses on Adam and Eve are softened:

> They shall not labour in vain,
>   or bear children for calamity;
> for they shall be the offspring of the blessed of the Lord,
>   and their children with them.
>
> (Isa. 65: 23)

A man's toil (Gen. 3: 17–19) will always result in success; and a woman's labour pains (3: 16) will always be blessed with the birth of a perfect child. Only the serpent's curse remains unaffected (Isa. 65: 25).

Finally, liberation theologians share with Marxists the belief that eschatology and politics are inseparable. It has been said that the Marxists have taken over from the Church that urgent expectation that was so characteristic of early Christianity: the belief that the Kingdom of God was at hand, and a commitment to working towards bringing in the new age. Certainly the liberation theologians have recovered the Utopian vision of biblical prophecy and early Christianity, and urge Christians to work here and now towards its fulfilment. The vision of a new age, where 'they shall sit every man under his own vine and under his fig-tree, and none shall make them afraid' (Mic. 4: 4), must be verified in social praxis, to use Marxist jargon.

So powerful are the vision and the commitment and the sense of solidarity with the poor that, where political action seems to be incapable of bringing down evil governments, and violence seems to be the only way left, then passages like Isa. 51: 22–3, Daniel 7, and Luke 1: 51 ff., quoted above, give comfort and support to Christians caught up in a revolutionary situation where radical changes in social structures, in Europe as well as the Third World, are needed. Then the visions of the biblical prophets have an extraordinary relevance.

The fact that it is a woman that utters those revolutionary words from the Magnificat quoted above (Luke 1; cf. also 1 Samuel 2), has been an inspiration to another fertile branch of modern Christian exegesis, namely feminist interpretation. Although for many women the Bible as a whole is irredeemably 'patriarchal', with little or nothing to say to their situation in society today, there have been some successful attempts to discover or rediscover relevant language and imagery, till now neglected by predominantly male interpreters within a predominantly male institution. Thus there is a new emphasis on the role of women prophets like Miriam, mentioned on equal terms with Moses and Aaron (Mic. 6: 4), and Deborah, perhaps 'woman of fire' rather than 'wife of Lappidoth' (Judg. 4: 4).

Passages about an unnamed young woman who had more faith than the king of Judah (Isa. 7: 14), and Lilith, Adam's first wife who would not submit to him (cf. Isa. 34: 14 NRSV), receive fresh scholarly attention, as does the 'daughter of Zion' image (e.g. 37: 22; 49: 14 ff.; 52: 1 f.; 54: 1–10; 66: 7 ff.), which is almost as prominent in Isaiah as the traditionally more familiar 'servant of the Lord'. The rare occasions when female images are applied to God (e.g. Isa. 42: 14; 45: 10; 49: 14 f.; 66: 13) take on a new significance as well. Feminist interpreters have also noted that Jesus, in his interpretation of Isaiah 61: 1–2, quoted above, chooses a woman to illustrate what is meant by 'the oppressed' (Luke 4: 16–30).

Anyone interested in prophecy and fulfilment, or anyone seeking to understand 'prophecy and the Prophets' within the context of the community that canonized them, cannot afford to turn a blind eye to these most recent stages in the history of interpretation.

BIBLIOGRAPHY

General

Blenkinsopp, J., *A History of Prophecy in Israel* (Westminster Press, Philadelphia 1983, and SPCK, London 1984)

Clements, R. E., *Prophecy and Tradition* (Basil Blackwell, Oxford 1975)

Coggins, R. J., A. Phillips and M. A. Knibb, eds., *Israel's Prophetic Tradition* (Cambridge University Press, Cambridge 1982)

Encyclopaedia Judaica, 16 vols. (Keter, Jerusalem 1971)

Heaton, E. W., *The Old Testament Prophets* (rev. edn., Darton, Longman & Todd, London 1977)

Heschel, A. J., *The Prophets* (Harper, New York 1957)

Hill, D., *New Testament Prophecy* (Marshall, Morgan & Scott, London 1979)

Jewish Encyclopaedia, 12 vols. (Funk & Wagnall, New York 1901)

Lang, B., *Monotheism and the Prophetic Minority: An Essay in Biblical History and Sociology* (Almond Press, Sheffield 1983)

Lindblom, J., *Prophecy in Ancient Israel* (Basil Blackwell, Oxford 1962)

Petersen, D. L. (ed.), *Prophecy in Israel* (SPCK London 1986)

Sandmel, S., *The Hebrew Scriptures: An Introduction to their Literature and Religious Ideas* (Oxford University Press, Oxford 1978)

Sawyer, J. F. A., *From Moses to Patmos* (SPCK, London 1977)

Scholem, G., *Major Trends in Jewish Mysticism* (Schocken, New York 1961)

Scott, R. B. Y., *The Relevance of the Prophets* (rev. edn., Macmillan, London 1968)

von Rad, G., *The Message of the Prophets* (SCM, London 1968)

Wilson, R. R., *Prophecy and Society in Ancient Israel* (Fortress Press, Philadelphia 1980)

The phenomenon of Prophecy

Berger, P. L., 'Charisma and Religious Innovation: The Social Location of Israelite Prophecy', *American Sociological Review* 28 (1963), 940–50

Carroll, R. P., *When Prophecy Fails* (Seabury Press, New York 1979)

Crenshaw, J. L., *Prophetic Conflict: Its Effect upon Israelite Religion* (de Gruyter, Berlin 1971)

Guillaume, A., *Prophecy and Divination* (Hodder & Stoughton, London 1938)

Johnson, A. R., *The Cultic Prophet and Israel's Psalmody* (University of Wales, Cardiff 1979)

Moran, W. L., 'New Evidence from Mari on the History of Prophecy', *Biblica* 50 (1969), 15–56

Overholt, T., 'Seeing is Believing: The Social Setting of Prophetic Acts of Power', *JSOT* 23 (1982), 3–31

Petersen, D. L., *The Roles of Israel's Prophets* (JSOT Press, Sheffield 1981)

Stacey, W. D., *Prophetic Drama in the Old Testament* (Epworth, London 1990)

Wilson, R. R., 'Prophecy and Ecstasy', *JBL* 98 (1979), 321–37

The Prophetic Literature

Clements, R. E., 'Patterns in the Prophetic Canon' in *Canon and Authority*, ed. G. W. Coats and B. O. Long (Fortress Press, Philadelphia 1977), 42–55

Gerstenberger, E., 'The Woe-oracles of the Prophets', *JBL* 81 (1962), 249–63

Habel, N., 'The Form and Significance of the Call Narrative', *ZAW* 77 (1965), 297–323

Huffmon, H., 'The Covenant Lawsuit in the Prophets', *JBL* 78 (1959), 285–95

March, W. E., 'Prophecy' in *Old Testament Form Criticism*, ed. J. H. Hayes (Trinity University Press, San Antonio 1974), 141–77

Mowinckel, S., 'The Prophetic Word in the Psalms and the Prophetic Psalms' in *The Psalms in Israel's Worship*, II (Basil Blackwell, Oxford 1972), 53–73

Scott, R. B. Y., 'The Literary Structure of Isaiah's Oracles', *Studies in Old Testament Prophecy*, ed. H. H. Rowley (T. & T. Clark, Edinburgh 1950), 175–86

Westermann, C., *Basic Forms of Prophetic Speech* (Lutterworth, London 1976)

The Message of the Prophets

Barton, J., 'Understanding Old Testament Ethics', *JSOT* 9 (1978), 44–64

Eichrodt, W., *Theology of the Old Testament*, I (SCM Press, London 1968), 472–501

Miller, P. D., *Sin and Judgement in the Prophets* (Scholars' Press, Chico, California 1982)

Mowinckel, S., *He that Cometh* (Basil Blackwell, Oxford 1959)

Ollenburger, B. C., *Zion, the City of the Great King: A Theological Symbol of the Jerusalem Cult* (JSOT Press, Sheffield 1986)

Plöger, O., *Theocracy and Eschatology* (Basil Blackwell, Oxford 1968)

Porteous, N. W., 'The Basis of the Ethical Teaching of the Prophets' in *Living the Mystery* (Basil Blackwell, Oxford 1967), 47–60. Also in *Studies in Old Testament Prophecy*, ed. H. H. Rowley (T. & T. Clark, Edinburgh 1950), 143–56

Snaith, N. H., *The Distinctive Ideas of the Old Testament* (Epworth, London 1944)

von Rad, G., 'The Origin of the Concept of the Day of the Lord', *JSS* 4 (1959), 97–108

The Prophets (I): Moses to Huldah

Brueggemann, W., 'The Kerygma of the Deuteronomistic Historian', *Interpretation* 22 (1968), 387–402

Buber, M., *Moses: The Revelation and the Covenant* (East and West Library, Horovitz, London; Green, New York 1946)

Carroll, R. P., 'The Elijah-Elisha Sagas: Some Remarks on Prophetic Succession', *VT* 19 (1969), 400–15

Hoftijzer, J. and G. van der Kooij, *Aramaic Texts from Deir Alla* (E. J. Brill, Leiden 1976)

Jones, G. H., *I and II Kings* (Eerdmans, Grand Rapids; Marshall, Morgan and Scott, London 1985)

McKane, W., *Prophets and Wise Men* (SCM Press, London 1965)

Polzin, R., *Moses and the Deuteronomist* (Seabury Press, New York 1980)

Prickett, S., 'Towards a Rediscovery of the Bible: The Still Small Voice', in *Ways of Reading the Bible* (University of Sussex, Brighton 1981)

The Prophets (II): Isaiah, Jeremiah, and Ezekiel

Anderson, B. W., 'Exodus Typology in Second Isaiah' in *Israel's Prophetic Heritage*, ed. B. W. Anderson and W. Harrelson (SCM Press, London 1962), 1977–95

Brueggemann, W., 'Unity and Dynamic in the Isaiah Tradition', *JSOT* 29 (1984), 89–127

Carroll, R. P., *Jeremiah* (SCM Press, London 1986)

Clements, R. E., *Isaiah and the Deliverance of Jerusalem* (JSOT Press, Sheffield 1980)

Greenberg, M., *Ezekiel 1–20: A New Translation with Introduction and Commentary* (Doubleday, New York 1983)

Joyce, P., *Divine Initiative and Human Response in Ezekiel* (Sheffield Academic Press, Sheffield 1989)

Kaiser, O., *Isaiah 1–12* (Westminster Press, Philadelphia and SCM Press, revised edition (London 1983)

id., *Isaiah 13–39* (Westminster Press, Philadelphia and SCM Press, London 1974)

Mettinger, T., *A Farewell to the Servant Songs* (Gleerup, Lund 1983)

Nicholson, E. W., *Preaching to the Exiles* (Basil Blackwell, Oxford 1970)

Rowley, H. H., 'The Suffering Servant and the Davidic Messiah' in *The Servant of the Lord and Other Essays* (2nd edn., Basil Blackwell, Oxford 1965), 63–93

Sawyer, J. F. A., '"The Daughter of Zion" and the "Servant of the Lord" in Isaiah. A Comparison', *JSOT* 44 (1989), 89–107

Skinner, J., *Prophecy and Religion: Studies in the Life of Jeremiah* (Cambridge University Press, Cambridge 1955)

Westermann, C., *Isaiah 40–66* (Westminster Press, Philadelphia and SCM Press, London 1969)

Whitley, C. A., 'The Date of Jeremiah's Call', *VT* 14 (1964), 467–83

Zimmerli, W., *Ezekiel*, 2 vols. (Fortress Press, Philadelphia 1983 and 1985)

The Prophets (III): Daniel to Malachi

Ackroyd, P. R., *Israel under Babylon and Persia* (Clarendon Press, Oxford 1970)

Barton, J., *Amos's Oracles against the Nations* (Basil Blackwell, Oxford 1980)

Casey, M., *Son of Man: The Interpretation and Influence of Daniel 7* (SPCK, London 1979)

Eaton, J., *Obadiah, Nahum, Habakkuk and Zephaniah* (Macmillan, New York, and SCM Press, London 1961)

Hillers, D. R., *Micah: A Commentary on the Book of the Prophet Micah* (Fortress Press, Philadelphia 1983)

Jones, D. R., *Haggai, Zechariah and Malachi* (Macmillan, New York and SCM Press, London 1956)

Lacocque, A., *The Book of Daniel* (John Knox Press, Atlanta and SPCK, London 1979)

Landes, G. M., 'The Kerygma of the Book of Jonah', *Interpretation* 21 (1967), 1–31

Magonet, J., *Form and Meaning: Studies in Literary Techniques in the Book of Jonah* (Almond Press, Sheffield 1985)

Mays, J. L., *Hosea* (Westminster Press, Philadelphia and SCM Press, London 1969).

id., *Amos* (Westminster Press, Philadelphia and SCM Press, London 1969)

id., *Micah* (Westminster Press, Philadelphia and SCM Press, London 1983)

Petersen, D. L., *Haggai, Zechariah 1–8* (Westminster Press, Philadelphia and SCM Press, London 1985)

Porteous, N. W., *Daniel* (Westminster Press, Philadelphia and SCM Press, London 1965)

Wolff, H. W., *Hosea* (Fortress Press, Philadelphia 1974)
id., *Joel and Amos* (Fortress Press, Philadelphia 1977)
id., *Micah* (Augsburg Fortress Press, Minneapolis 1990)

Prophecy and Interpretation

Alexander, P. S., *Textual Sources for the Study of Judaism* (Manchester University Press, Manchester 1984)

Arberry, A. J., *The Koran Interpreted* (Oxford University Press, Oxford 1958)

Barrett, C. K., 'The Interpretation of the Old Testament in the New' in *Cambridge History of the Bible*, I (1970), 377–411

Barzel, H., 'The Last Prophet—The Biblical Ground of Bialik's Poetry', *Biblical Patterns in Modern Literature*, ed. D. H. Hirsch and N. Ashkenasy (Scholars' Press, Chico, California 1984)

Bell's Introduction to the Quran, ed. W. M. Watt (Edinburgh University Press, Edinburgh 1970)

Blenkinsopp, J., *Prophecy and Canon: A Contribution to the Study of Jewish Origins* (University of Notre Dame, Notre Dame 1977)

Brooke, G. J., *Exegesis at Qumran* (JSOT Press, Sheffield 1985)

Carmi, T. ed., *The Penguin Book of Hebrew Verse* (London 1981)

Childs, B. S., *Introduction to the Old Testament as Scripture* (Fortress Press, Philadelphia 1985)

Coggins, R. J. and Houlden, J. L. eds., *A Dictionary of Biblical Interpretation* (SCM Press, London 1990)

Cohn, N., *The Pursuit of the Millennium* (Paladin, London 1970)

Danby, H., *The Mishnah* (Oxford University Press, Oxford 1936)

Elliott, C., *Praying the Kingdom: Towards a Political Spirituality* (Darton, Longman & Todd, London 1985)

Ginzberg, L., *The Legends of the Jews*, 7 vols. (Jewish Publication Society, Philadelphia 1909); 1 vol. (New York 1956)

Gottwald, N. K., *Bible and Liberation: Political and Social Hermeneutics* (Seabury Press, New York 1983)

Gutierrez, G., *A Theology of Liberation* (SCM Press, London 1974)

Miranda, J. P., *Marx and the Bible: A Critique of the Philosophy of Oppression* (SCM Press, London 1977)

Parrinder, G., *Jesus in the Quran* (Barnes & Noble, New York 1965)

Ruether, R. R., *Sexism and God-Talk. Towards a Feminist Theology* (SCM Press, London 1983)

Russell, L. M. ed., *Feminist Interpretation of the Bible* (Basil Blackwell, Oxford 1985)

Sawyer, J. F. A., *The Fifth Gospel. Isaiah in the History of Christianity* (Cambridge University Press, Cambridge 1993)

Scholem, G., *The Messianic Idea in Judaism* (Schocken, New York 1971)

Shorter Encyclopaedia of Islam, ed. H. A. R. Gibb and J. H. Kramers (E. J. Brill, Leiden 1974)

Stenning, J., *The Targum of Isaiah* (Oxford University Press, Oxford 1949)

Stone, M., *Scriptures, Sects and Visions* (Fortress Press, Philadelphia 1980)

Trible, P., *God and the Rhetoric of Sexuality* (Fortress Press, Philadelphia 1978), 31–71

Vermes, G., *The Dead Sea Scrolls in English* (rev. edn., Penguin, London 1975)

id., 'Bible and Midrash: Early Old Testament Exegesis' in *Cambridge History of the Bible*, I (1970), 199–231

Abbreviations

JBL   *Journal of Biblical Literature* (Scholars' Press, Chico)

JSOT   *Journal for the Study of the Old Testament* (Sheffield)

JSS   *Journal of Semitic Studies* (Manchester University)

VT   *Vetus Testamentum* (E. J. Brill, Leiden)

ZAW   *Zeitschrift für die Alttestamentliche Wissenschaft* (Walter de Gruyter, Berlin and New York)

INDEX OF PASSAGES CITED

GENERAL INDEX